Seduce Your Customers

Seduce Your Customers

AN ENTREPRENEUR'S GUIDE TO MARKETING

Kerry Szymanski, M.B.A.

Enjoy!

Kerry

Kerry Communications Publishing
www.KerryCommunications.com

SEDUCE YOUR CUSTOMERS

Cover design: Glen M. Edelstein
Book design: Glen M. Edelstein

Library of Congress Catalog-in-Publishing Data
Printed in the United States of America

Contents

Acknowledgements

I'd like to thank all of the people that have encouraged me throughout the writing process. I'd like to thank Carol Killman Rosenberg and Jeremy Hawkins for their brilliant pens by assisting me in editing my book. Rosemary Matthews for her support, encouragement and endless hours of proofreading. Glen Edelstein for his patience, gorgeous cover and interior layout of the book. Ned Stone for his assistance with the title, and Collin Whitehead for his intellectual power. Joe Englander for his legal assistance and friendship. In addition, I'd like to thank my Dad, my brothers Dusty and Jason, Carmand Lucius, Dean Morrison, Steven Lafonte, Greg Pitts, Stephanie Robbins, Tas Salini, Carlos Santos, Peter West, Sheila Walden, Andre West, and many other friends for their unbridled support throughout my writing process. And a special thank you to all of my students who have inspired me to write the book. They are the reason that I get up and go to work every day and they bring a tremendous amount of joy to my life. Learning should be fun, and my hope is that this book will bring some clarity and levity to the world of marketing and branding. Enjoy!

Seduce Your Customers

Introduction

Looking for Brand Love in
All the Right Places

Branding and marketing a new product or service can be overwhelming. As an entrepreneur, your time and resources are limited, perhaps even maxed out. Effectively marketing your products or services may have even taken a backseat to everything else you need to do. Knowing where to start or what works (and what doesn't) requires a lot of homework, but you've probably been so busy playing various roles—salesperson, accountant, manufacturer, web designer, and even janitor—that you haven't been able to do the legwork.

But here's the simple truth: Effective branding and marketing are your keys to building a successful business. My goal in writing this book is to provide you with a guide to understanding the integral branding and marketing tools you'll need to build lifelong relationships with your customers. And I'm here to inspire you to make these important tasks your main priority. Entrepreneurship can be tough—there are a million tasks to juggle, and marketing often falls to a lower priority. My goal is to simplify these concepts and help you through the process so that you can live happily ever after with your customers.

Early in my career, I worked in corporate marketing for multi-million dollar companies. These opportunities taught me the fundamentals of marketing… but a corporate checkbook is often vastly different from the resources of a new entrepreneur. I later ventured into entrepreneurship as a handbag designer and boutique owner, and I started a successful business-consulting firm.

As an entrepreneur, I understand what it takes to market a business with limited resources. Over the past decade, I've been sharing my business knowledge as a college professor, teaching marketing principles to future entrepreneurs. Initially, marketing fundamentals can seem obscure and ambiguous, just as finding Prince Charming and falling in love can seem like elusive goals. But it doesn't have to be a mystery.

I've written *Seduce Your Customers*—a combination of love stories and marketing principles—to help you better understand the importance of each stage of marketing in building better relationships with your customers. Essentially, the best way to attract and retain customers is to use the same tools that people use (or at least that people *should* use) when falling in love and starting a romantic relationship.

For example, when you experience "love at first sight," you're blown away by physical attraction and by how magically fortunate you are to have been in the right place at the right time to meet that *perfect person*. The same principles hold true for attracting new customers. Your brand must be

(1) extremely attractive and (2) located in the right place at the right time, so that it makes new customers feel enraptured enough to buy your product or service.

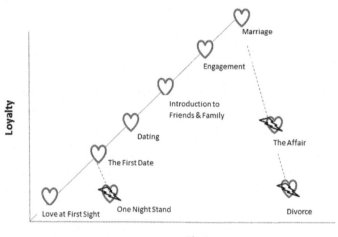

I've broken down the phases of marketing into the different stages of courtship, diagramed above on the *Dating Lifecycle Curve.*

The *Dating Lifecycle Curve* illustrates the various stages of falling in love, and each stage correlates to a specific phase in the marketing of your business. This simple and fun analogy demonstrates, for example, why you want to get "married" to your customers, rather than falling into a "One Night Stand," "Affair," or "Divorce."

However, unlike most romantic relationships, entrepreneurs are dating many people at the same time: their customers. You're constantly on the prowl to attract and seduce new customers, while also trying to maintain loyalty with your existing customers. As the *Dating Lifecycle Curve* illustrates, the longer a customer "dates" your brand, the stronger their loyalty becomes.

After a brief introduction of marketing principles in Chapter 1, Chapter 2 provides an overview of the *Dating Lifecycle Curve* and its relationship to marketing. Then, the chapters that follow will correlate to each phase of the *Dating Lifecycle Curve* and offer advice on how to use marketing and branding concepts to attract and retain customers. Each chapter is broken down into sections that will help you best utilize marketing strategies to increase brand loyalty for your business, whether it's a retail store, website, product or service. I also provide tips on how to use advertising and social media to increase customer loyalty. At the end of the book, I've included a glossary of marketing and dating terminology as they relate to branding your business.

Simply put, branding is a process that takes time. It's also an essential factor that helps determine the success of your business. **Branding** is defined as the "who," that is, the process of creating and developing your company's image over time. I'll explain how to create an effective and consistent brand image in Chapter 1. **Marketing** is the "what, when, where and how." It is the planning and implementation of ideas that will increase sales for your business. Developing a strong marketing strategy helps business owners decide what they're going to sell, where they're going to sell it, and how they're going to promote what they are offering. Throughout the book, I'll detail techniques that will help you create a strong desire for your brand and attract new customers.

But creating desire is only the starting point. As an entrepreneur, you'll need to cultivate loyal relationships using effective marketing tactics that appeal to your customers at

SEDUCE YOUR CUSTOMERS 15

various stages throughout your relationship. Your goal is to build long-term relationships with your customers that evoke emotions of attachment and loyalty that mirror a marriage. This book will help you to simplify the marketing process by applying the principles of seduction and romance to your marketing strategies that will lead to life-long customer relationships. Congratulations on taking your first steps to better understanding how customers fall in love with your brand and creating the opportunity for loyalty to increase in all of your relationships.

Chapter 1

Getting Ready to Date—
Reviewing the Basics of Branding

Why do *you* buy certain brands? Do you like the packaging? Is it on sale? Is it a status symbol? Does it taste good? In today's marketplace, consumers have a plethora of choices. So what makes them choose one brand over another? Answering this question for yourself will help increase your sales, because you'll better understand what motivates your customers to become loyal to you.

Marketing your brand is a lot like falling in love. Remember the last time you saw someone who made your heart skip a beat? Perhaps it was an actor on television, a super-model or a rock star. They are the images that gloss the covers of magazines, movies, billboards and television shows around the world and embody just a few of the attributes that the advertising industry has deemed beautiful, attractive and sexy.

With these images of beauty and attraction preconditioned into our culture, our society's affinity toward how someone "looks" is undeniable. If advertising preconditions us to believe that we should be attracted to humans who are physically beautiful, entrepreneurs can utilize this theory of human attraction to create marketing vehicles that are "tall, dark and handsome" or a "blonde bombshell."

> **Love Note:** *It's important to create lust and desire for your brand when new customers first interact with your product or service. However, in order to sustain that relationship, you'll need to implement marketing techniques that foster a long-term relationship.*

CREATING LOVE FOR YOUR BRAND

Take a moment to think about your relationship with your favorite brands. Are you "happily married" to this brand? Have you recently had an "affair" with a competitor's product or service because you received a coupon in the mail? Did you try something new because you were infatuated with the competitor's packaging? And have you ever had a one-night stand with a product because your first experience was so bad that it immediately became your last?

It is your job as a business owner to ensure that your customers resist the temptation to jump ship the first time a better offer appears. And for this reason, it's important to think about your brand as a spouse. In real life, when couples marry, they never intentionally set out to cheat on one other or to get divorced—and many of the best couples never do. As an entrepreneur, it should be your mission to create that same sense of loyalty—that perfect marriage—with your customers. They should be so in love with your product that cheating is absolutely out of the question!

So where do you begin? First, we need to get you ready for your first date by better understanding a concept called the **Attraction Factor.**

The Attraction Factor takes into account a person's innate physical desires, which is the first step in their metamorphosis into a deeper relationship. This metamorphosis mirrors the phases of humans falling in love—moving from an initial physical desire to a true emotional connection. Branding and advertising can be highly successful if you follow these same steps. The first step is to understand your customers' physical desires, and to implement marketing tactics that will seduce and attract them to your brand. Once you understand the different stages of a customer's falling in love with your brand, you'll then be able to implement marketing tactics that will secure their loyalty and lead to a long-term relationship.

Your first goal should always be to have your customers fall in love with you. For example, when you go on a first date with someone and there isn't a connection, you probably won't go on a second date. Similarly, customers need to feel connected to your brand from the very first date. This realization is important because it shows the importance of the customer's first interaction, and his or her connection with your brand. So, you must put significant time and effort into preparing for that first date; it's crucial to offer customers the first-date experience they were hoping for in order to achieve that all-important second date.

Michael met Caroline through an online dating website. They emailed and chatted on the phone a few times to get to know one another. Michael had a sultry voice and was very articulate. His profile stated that he was 6'1", had dark hair and hazel eyes, and was a fit 40-year-old professional. After speaking on the phone, Caroline and Michael realized they had a lot in common, and they decided to meet for coffee over the weekend. Caroline was so excited to meet someone her own age who shared many of her interests and values. Even before meeting him, she was falling for Michael.

Caroline arrived at the café right on time. She looked around and didn't see Michael anywhere. In the corner of the café, a 60-year-old man who was approximately 5'6 was waving his hand and shouting her name. At first, she wondered if she knew him from work or the neighborhood, but then she realized that this man... this imposter... was Michael!

Needless to say, Michael never got a second date...

BOREDOM

Alternatively, long-term customers can easily become bored with your brand, and they might try another brand if their excitement with, or loyalty to, your brand is wavering. Customers can easily "cheat," and they're not likely to feel any sense of remorse.

Boredom is said to be the number one reason why people cheat in their romantic relationships. With that in mind, if you want to build a long-term relationship with your customers, it's important to treat your existing customers like gold. Remember, regular customers are your bedrock. They are the ones keeping you in business. Many entrepreneurs take their existing customers for granted and spend too much time trying to attract new customers. Think about it: If you focus more energy on your existing customers and provide them with products and services that make them feel special, they'll continue to feel loyal to your brand. It's much easier and less expensive to retain existing customers than it is to attract new ones.

> **Love Note:** *Treat your existing customers like gold. They are your bread and butter. If you develop products and customer experiences that are unparalleled in your industry, you'll develop long-term relationships with your customers. Show them that you appreciate them with loyalty and thank you programs.*

IDENTIFYING YOUR TARGET CUSTOMERS

In order to build a relationship with a customer, you must first understand who wants to date you and potentially engage in a relationship with your brand. In the dating world, everyone has a list of the internal and external qualities of their perfect mate. Perhaps your ideal date is someone who is tall, funny, intelligent, honest and kindhearted. Entrepreneurs should develop a similar list in order to determine which customers are right for them. Identifying your **Target Customers**, that is, the people most likely to buy your products and services, will help you to develop marketing tactics that are seductive, compelling and cost effective.

I often ask entrepreneurs, "Who is your target customer?" Many answer, "Everyone!" But I'm here to tell you that "everyone" is *not* your target customer. That's like saying that you could go out with "anyone" on a date and make them fall in love with you! Creating marketing initiatives that target "everyone" is not only time-consuming, but also very expensive, and likely futile.

Many entrepreneurs also make the critical mistake of believing that they *themselves* are the target customer. Do all of your customers look and act as you do? Sometimes this is true; many times it isn't. Understanding your target customer is crucial to the success of your business. Once your business is up and running, your target customers may surprise you. So it's important to stay flexible and adapt to the changing needs of your customers.

> *When Fiona first opened her women's clothing boutique, she only bought clothes that she liked and that she would wear. She was 31 years old, single and college educated. She lived in a large city and had an average income of $75K/year. She liked to work out, go to upscale bars and restaurants, participate in triathlons, and walk her dog. However, during her first year of business, many of her customers turned out to be older and much more conservative than she was. After the first year in business, Fiona changed her merchandising strategy and started buying clothes that would appeal to her older, more conservative clientele. She also changed where she advertised, hosted wine and cheese parties, and partnered with local charities. Her new strategy worked so well that, by her fourth year in business, she had opened a second retail location.*

There are often several groups who may be potential customers. These groups are known as **Target Customer Profiles**. Defining your Target Customer Profiles will help you identify the right merchandise, the right marketing vehicles, the right location, and the right price that will appeal to your target customers. For example, if you're opening a children's clothing boutique in a suburban location, your intended customers will most likely be "moms." However, "moms" is still too vague to describe your target customer. Probing deeper, there are additional questions you must ask yourself:

- How old is she?
- Where does she live?
- Does she work?
- What is her annual income?

These characteristics are known as demographics. **Demographics** are used to help define your target customer and are based on criteria such as age, income, occupation, marital status, gender, religion, ethnicity, education and family status. And like it or not, we often do the same thing in dating. For example, the demographic profile of your perfect date might be someone who is single, between 30 and 40 years old, earns an average of $50,000 per year, has at least a bachelor's degree, and works in a professional field.

Another tool that can help you identify your target customers is psychographic data. **Psychographics** are the attitudes, values and beliefs of your target customer. Applying this to dating, perhaps you value someone who is active, enjoys movies, and spends time with their friends on the weekends.

In regards to business, some questions you might ask yourself when defining the psychographics of your target customer are:

- What motivates your target customer?
- What type of lifestyle do they lead?
- What are their activities and interests?
- What values are important to them? Money? Status? Family?

> **Love Note:** *"Everyone" is not your target customer.* Create two or three Target Customer Profiles to help you with decisions in advertising, merchandising and customer service offerings.

Whether you're just starting a new company or would like to expand your current brand, it's important to develop your Target Customer Profiles. These quickly reference demographic and psychographic details, and include a picture of the customers who represent your target customer segments. Target Customer Profiles are helpful when deciding upon things like:

- Where to advertise
- Which social media platforms to use
- Which services are important to your customers
- What types of merchandise, sizing, colors, etc. your target customer will prefer
- What type of music you should play in your store

Once you understand your Target Customer Profiles, you'll be able to make efficient and effective decisions to help improve your business and increase sales.

UNDERSTANDING KEY TERMS

Before moving forward, I would like to define some key terms that will be used throughout this book. These terms are also listed in the glossary at the end of the book to provide you with references as needed.

"Brand" and Related Terms

Your **Brand** is that unique quality that identifies your product, service or company, such as a name, word, logo or design. For example, the word "Nike" identifies the company Nike, Inc. The "swoosh" logo also represents the company and often stands alone, because Nike, Inc. has devoted years of consistent advertising with the "swoosh" on its clothing, television commercials, magazine ads, retail stores, shopping bags, hang tags, sponsored athletes, and more.

Brands are made up of various elements such as:

- Name
- Logo
- Tagline
- Scent
- Sound
- Taste

Branding is the "who" of your business. It is the *process* of creating and developing your company's image over time. Successful branding is accomplished by having a consistent and memorable company name, logo, product offering, etc., and the process of branding helps create a positive impression about your company and its offerings. As an entrepreneur, you are constantly managing how your customers perceive your brand, also known as your **Brand Image.**

In business, it's imperative to develop a strong brand in order to expand your business and increase sales. What's important to remember is that building a brand is a slow process. It takes time, consistency and acute marketing skills in order to successfully build a strong brand name. Some companies invest large sums of money in marketing to swiftly build their brand name. However, many of these companies fail to realize that in order to be successful, their marketing campaigns must be consistent and memorable, while also building an emotional connection with their target customers.

If you are an entrepreneur without a large marketing budget, I have good news. You can still create a strong brand through a variety of tools such as:

- A memorable name
- A catchy logo
- Consistent use of brand colors on all packaging, hang tags, signage, etc.
- Consistent use of font for the logo
- A great location
- Superior products
- Exemplary service
- Strong community partnerships
- Skillful use of social media platforms
- Dazzling design on all company marketing vehicles, including ads, email newsletters, business cards and websites

Marketing

Marketing is the "what, when, where and how" of your business. It's the planning and implementation of ideas that will help increase sales. A strong marketing strategy helps business owners decide what they're going to sell and how they're going to promote it. It also helps them determine the best time and place to reach their target customers. These places are known as **Distribution Channels,** which can be defined as any point of sale opportunity. Distribution channels include retail stores, outlet stores, ecommerce websites, mobile phone apps, catalogs, infomercials, kiosks, selling opportunities through Facebook, art festivals, flea markets, and much more. Many businesses utilize multiple distribution channels, such as a retail store *and* an ecommerce website. Your marketing strategy should not only decide the distribution channels where consumers can purchase your products and services, it should also determine which specific products and services to offer, and at what price.

Advertising

Advertising is a vital subset of marketing. It involves promoting a company's products and brand image through magazines, television, websites, signage, social media, Internet, billboards, bus wraps, etc.

You can use advertising to attract attention and increase sales. With so many choices of where to advertise, it's imperative that you understand your target customer and how they spend their leisure time. Do they spend a significant amount of time watching television, reading magazines, surfing the internet or social media sites? Is a television commercial the best way to advertise your brand, or would an advertisement in a magazine, online or a social media site produce better results? And which one can you afford? Advertising can be expensive. A solid marketing plan helps you decide where you should advertise, what message you should feature in you advertisement, and how often you should advertise.

The ultimate goal of any business is to increase sales through new and repeat customers. Businesses strive to gain new customers and convert them into loyal, long-term customers. If we look at branding, marketing and advertising in terms of dating, we realize that there is a direct correlation between (1) time and (2) loyalty when developing romantic relationships. As time increases in a relationship, so does the level of loyalty. When couples first meet, they may not be interested in pursuing a serious relationship. Each may even be dating a few different people. Loyalty at this stage is not very strong because very little time has been invested in the relationship.

Couples who start dating exclusively, become engaged, and eventually get married have formed a very loyal bond. If we apply this concept to marketing, we see that the longer a consumer buys your brand, the stronger their loyalty grows. However, if you don't continue to cherish your long-term customers and create new products and experiences to keep them interested, their loyalty may diminish. If this happens, they could easily "cheat" on you by having an affair with a competitor's brand. So, the longer your customers interact with your brand, the stronger and more creative your marketing strategies will need to be in order to sustain your long-term relationship.

> **Love Note:** *The correlation between time and loyalty holds true in both marketing and romantic relationships. The longer a consumer continues to buy a brand, the stronger their loyalty to that brand grows, as long as their needs are met.*

The best examples of customers who have a strong sense of loyalty are those who have been in relationships with brands since childhood. Think about brands that you have been using since you were a child. Are you using a certain brand of toothpaste, peanut butter or toilet paper because you grew up with it? Was it something your parents purchased, so you feel comfortable with, and loyal to, that brand?

Understanding the emotions that motivate customers to maintain their loyalty will help you create loyal customers. Once you understand the fundamental appeal of your company (what makes you seductive) and what drives customers to purchase your brand, you will be able to create advertising campaigns, new products, and new services that not only meet the needs of your customers, but also exceed their wildest expectations.

Social Media

In today's marketplace, social media is redefining how companies develop and maintain relationships with their customers. The very essence of social media is about building relationships. Many novice entrepreneurs think social media is a free venue where they can promote their products and services. And yes, social media is a wonderful platform upon which to share information about your brand. But there are a million other companies competing against you, and success at social media marketing is not as simple as regularly updating your Facebook and Twitter pages.

Social media has changed the way companies market themselves by opening a direct channel to their customers. Traditional television, print, radio and billboard ads provide a one-way conversation with consumers. But social media allows for a two-way conversation. Facebook, Twitter, Pinterest, Instagram and Foursquare are all popular social media platforms at the time of the writing of this book. However, new social media evolves at lightning speed, and new platforms are launching daily. It's important to understand which social media platforms your customers use, and which ones will best fit your brand.

So don't be shy! Building engaging relationships with your customers through social media will increase loyalty to your brand, because your customers will feel they are part of your business. For example, many businesses are afraid to let their customers post on their Facebook page because they worry about negative comments. However, many cable and phone companies have embraced this as a way to satisfy disgruntled customers. These companies contact unhappy customers and turn their negative experience into a positive one, and next thing you know, the customer has posted a new comment about the amazing customer service the company bestowed upon them.

It's important to understand that social media is all about building a relationship with your customers. I've met entrepreneurs who employ their children to post information on social media platforms because they're scared of new technology, or because they believe they don't have time to dedicate to learning this form of marketing. But don't be scared —go ahead and jump on the bandwagon! Learn the new technology, and you'll quickly realize that you'll be able to develop stronger relationships with your customers.

*   *   *

Understanding who your target customers are will help you to make better branding, marketing and advertising decisions. You can utilize marketing strategies to plan and implement ideas to grow your business, and to develop successful advertising to promote your brand. However, these strategies might differ whether you're trying to attract or retain customers. Remember, the longer a customer "dates" your brand, the stronger their loyalty grows. The next chapter will explain the *Dating Lifecycle Curve*, which will help you create marketing strategies to attract and retain loyal customers.

Chapter 2

Falling In and Out of Love— Comparing Marketing to Relationships

Now that you understand the direct correlation between time and loyalty when building a relationship with your customer, you should also understand how important it is to nurture your customers just as you would nurture a romantic relationship.

The longer a customer "dates" your brand, the more likely they are to become loyal to it, perhaps even to the extent of metaphorically "marrying" your brand. For example, we all know people who are avid Coke or Pepsi drinkers. They are committed to one or the other, and they never cheat on their favorite brand, regardless of the circumstances. They see themselves as being in a happy, healthy, rewarding marriage— and nothing the competition does can make the grass look greener on the other side.

In order to illustrate this point, I've created the *Dating Lifecycle Curve* (see the next page), which shows the different stages of a customer's relationship with any brand. The *Dating Lifecycle Curve* is an analogy of the marketing and branding process; the curve represents the progressive phases of romantic relationships, as well as the necessary components of successful marketing and branding.

There are nine different stages during which a customer becomes more or less involved in their relationship with your brand. By applying appropriate marketing and branding strategies at each stage of the *Dating Lifecycle Curve*, you'll be successful in developing a long-term relationship with your customers.

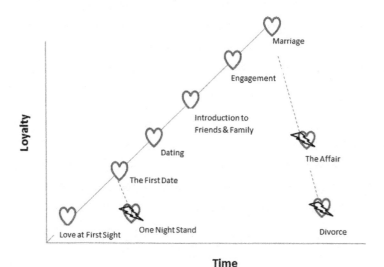

THE DATING LIFECYCLE CURVE

The remainder of this book takes an in-depth look at each stage of the *Dating Lifecycle Curve*. Each chapter corresponds to one stage, and I'll explain how you can develop a deep emotional bond with your customers through marketing and branding strategies that differ depending upon the amount of time the customer has invested in your brand. Again, the more time a customer invests in your brand, the more their loyalty to your brand will increase, as long as you continue to meet or exceed their needs at each stage.

> **Love Note:** *The Dating Lifecycle Curve illustrates the various stages of a romantic relationship as an analogy to marketing your business. Marketing techniques should differ in each stage, just as dating strategies change at different phases of a romantic relationship.*

As in most romantic relationships, not every business relationship is a smooth and easy ride. Sometimes things go wrong. The chapters "One Night Stand," "The Affair," and "Divorce" will help you analyze why you might be losing customers, and how to win them back. By looking at business in terms of dating, it's easier to understand why people become excited about a new brand, and what might make them decide to start dating someone else. Let's glance briefly at each phase of the *Dating Lifecycle Curve* in the sections below before taking a more in-depth look chapter-by-chapter.

Love at First Sight

This is where it all begins. Two people see each other across a crowded room and *va va voom!* Lightning strikes! An initial attraction based on internal desire is ignited by external beauty. The feeling is thrilling and intoxicating. It's the stuff movies are made of. Seduction in action.

Love at First Sight represents the acquisition phase in marketing. Your job during this phase is to create such an attractive presentation of your product or service that the customer won't be able to resist when they spot you across that crowded room. Because no time or loyalty has been invested with your brand at this point, many customers might choose to buy your brand based purely upon emotional and physical impulses. Seduction is understanding how to appeal to your target customers. Knowing this can help you, the business owner, create attractive logos, products, services, packaging, storefronts, websites and advertisements in order to appeal to new customers. It's also important for your brand to be available to the consumer through a variety of distribution channels, as well as introduced to new consumers through targeted advertisements. Chapter 3 will guide your marketing decisions with the goal of creating an initial "wow" factor, as well as ensuring that your brand is easily available to as many new customers as possible.

The First Date

A first date gives two people the opportunity to meet and become acquainted. In essence, they are interviewing one another to ascertain if they want to move on to a second date… and perhaps more.

There is a lot at stake during *The First Date* phase, because consumers are examining and testing your product/service for the first time. They are deciding if you are a good fit for them, and if there is the potential for a long-term relationship. Basically, this is a trial period that enables the consumer to get to know your brand. Your goal during this phase should be to create a memorable first experience so that the consumer wants to come back for a second date. In Chapter 4, I'll provide tips on how to create a remarkable first date experience. For example, you could offer free samples, trial sizes, compelling discounts, coupons and other marketing strategies. These and other tactics will ensure that the customer has a great first date with your brand, and will want to come back for more.

One-Night Stand

Unfortunately, some first dates turn into one-night stands. If this happens, it's important to ask yourself what went wrong. Why was the consumer only interested in a one-night stand and not in a relationship? Most of the time, the *One-Night Stand* phase occurs because the consumer simply didn't enjoy the first date with your brand. Both time and loyalty were minimal at that point, and if their first experience was a disaster (or even just subpar), then the consumer had no reason to give your brand a second chance.

It's important for you to avoid the *One-Night Stand* phase at all costs! To do this, identify the needs of your customers and the unique benefits your brand provides them. Remember: Every first date *must* be outstanding. In Chapter 5, I'll explain how you can achieve a great first date by focusing on quality and customer service. I'll also describe the pitfalls that some entrepreneurs face when trying to develop a new brand that may lead to a one-night stand. Once you are aware of these potential pitfalls, you'll be well equipped to avoid this dangerous phase of the *Dating Lifecycle Curve.*

Dating

This is a critical stage of evaluation for the consumer. Even though your customer had a great first date and agreed to a second date, you still need to "wow" them each and every time they encounter your product/service. However, because it's still early in the relationship, consumers may still be dating multiple brands and may not yet have a very strong sense of loyalty. Your job at this point is to create a marketing strategy that will help you draw the customer from the *Dating* phase into a much more serious relationship. In order to accomplish this, it is essential that you clearly identify your strengths, and how these strengths help meet your customer's needs. This will help you clearly define your particular competitive advantage, that is, what makes you better than the competition. In Chapter 6, you'll also learn how to expand your availability so consumers will be able to interact with you at a variety of venues and locations.

Introduction to Friends and Family

At this point in the relationship, loyalty and time begin to increase at the same rate. In the *Introduction to Friends and Family* phase, the customer that you are happily "dating" will now invite friends and family to try your brand, extending the scope of the relationship. This is a crucial point in the *Dating Lifecycle Curve*, because loyal customers can often become a brand's virtual sales force.

Every entrepreneur dreams that word-of-mouth marketing will be their ticket to increased sales. However, word-of-mouth marketing is hard to count on because it is very difficult to control. Nevertheless if your customers continue to have great experiences while dating your brand, they will be eager to tell their friends and family all about their exciting new relationship… and their enthusiasm will motivate their friends and family to go out on a first date with your brand as well.

Social media has taken this stage of marketing to an entirely new level. In Chapter 7, you'll learn tips on expanding your customer base, while also rewarding your current customers for their help in spreading the word about your brand.

Engagement

Loyalty often becomes "official" during the *Engagement* phase through various symbols. For example, when couples become engaged, a ring is given as a symbol of loyalty. When a customer becomes "engaged" to your brand, you may give them a loyalty card as a form of an engagement ring. Many companies offer loyalty cards or frequent-user programs to promote customer devotion. By this point, your customer has invested a significant amount of time with your brand, and they are falling in love with it. Still, during this phase, marketing efforts need to remain strong, because consumers still expect superior quality and exemplary service. In Chapter 8, you'll learn about various online and offline loyalty programs that will help you keep your customers engaged and thinking about marriage. You'll also learn how to implement loyalty programs and customer appreciation programs that will continue to make you irresistible to your customers.

Marriage

As a relationship grows stronger, loyalty and love increase over time and, hopefully, will result in marriage. Marriage is the highest point on the *Dating Lifecycle Curve* because it represents the point where consumers have invested highly in your brand, and they are now committed for life. But just like any marriage, your job is not finished after the wedding day. To maintain a high level of customer loyalty, it's important to continue innovating in order to keep excitement in the marriage. You can do this by adding new products, new distribution channels, or new marketing vehicles. In Chapter 9, I'll show you ways to keep your customers happily "married" by offering them consistent and exemplary products/services, while also constantly re-inventing yourself through various forms of innovation.

Affair

There are many reasons why consumers cheat on their favorite brands. Boredom, lack of communication, and lower price points are all reasons why your "married" customers might be tempted to cheat on you and find a brand that better suits their needs. But you can avoid the *Affair* phase by keeping the relationship exciting and by having excellent communication strategies. In Chapter 10, you'll learn how to keep your customers from cheating by implementing innovative marketing programs, increasing your availability and attractiveness, and developing creative pricing strategies.

Divorce

The *Divorce* phase represents the unwanted end of the relationship with your most loyal customers. You'll notice that customers are divorcing your brand because there will be a significant decline in repeat business. In order to avoid this phase, you need to monitor your relationships with your loyal customers while they are still "married" to your brand, and you need to be flexible enough to make changes when necessary. By implementing customer feedback mechanisms through surveys and focus groups, you'll be able to better meet and exceed your customer's continued needs and bring the love back into your marriage.

THE KEY "A" FACTORS – ATTRACTION, AVAILABILITY AND ASSETS

All entrepreneurs aspire to build a successful business that will be around for many years. To achieve a steady and lucrative income, you must understand what it takes to keep your customers happy in their relationship with you. Once you understand how to attract new customers while also keeping current customers in a state of bliss, you'll be able to effectively market your brand without wasting time or money. To accomplish this, three factors are crucial to varying degrees at each phase of the *Dating Lifecycle Curve*. I call these the Key "A" Factors: Attractiveness, Availability, and your brand's Assets.

For example, attractive packaging (Attraction) and product placement (Availability) are paramount during the *Love at First Sight* phase, as well as during subsequent phases throughout the *Dating Lifecycle Curve*. If Attraction and Availability are forgotten during the *Marriage* phase, some customers will be swayed by other more attractive or available brands. Product taste, value, quality, reliability and durability (Assets) are important in every phase after the *First Date*, and any faltering in a brand's Assets during these phases may lead to a *One-Night Stand* or an *Affair*.

Key "A" Factor #1: Attraction

Attraction is defined by the physical or visible attributes of your brand. It is important to consider the visual elements of your brand when first creating a new product or service. The design of a retail store or office will often determine whether or not a new customer walks through the front door. Attraction must be taken into consideration in all aspects of a product or service, including package design, advertisements, signage, mobile and tablet sites, websites, apps, catalogs, retail store designs, billboards, event marketing and public relations campaigns. This also applies to all social media forums such as Facebook, Twitter, Pinterest, Instagram, blogs, LinkedIn, Foursquare, YouTube and others. Ensuring all aspects of your brand are attractive helps you to seduce new customers and remind existing customers why they fell in love with your brand.

> **Love Note:** *Attractiveness must be predominant in every aspect of your brand. Everything a customer sees should evoke strong feelings of attraction and desire.*

Key "A" Factor #2: Availability

Availability involves both (1) the location and (2) the price points of a brand.

When first creating your company, you want to be sure that your brand is accessible to the consumer. Location, location, location! Your brand must be easy to find, whether it's by searching for your website online, driving to your retail location, or purchasing your brand in an otherwise cluttered store.

> **Love Note:** *Availability ensures that your products and services are available at the right place and at the right price.*

Key "A" Factor #3: Assets

As in dating, people are defined by both their internal and external qualities. The Assets of a brand are defined as the internal attributes and charactersitics of your product or service. Examples of a brand's Assets include reliability, durability, service, taste, quality and value.

Your customers have an expectation of what the experience will be like with your brand, and it's up to you to meet and exceed those expectations. Everything you do should deliver excellence each and every time a consumer interacts with your brand. Once a consumer starts dating your brand, your brand's Assets will become a determining factor in their decision to develop a long-term relationship with you.

> **Love Note:** *The Assets of your brand will determine whether or not a customer engages in a long-term relationship with your brand.*

Keeping the Key "A" Factors in Mind

As mentioned above, one or more of the Key "A" Factors will have more influence on the consumer's behavior at different phases of the *Dating Lifecycle Curve*. What does this mean for you? The answer is simple, and you can use the insights in the chapters that follow to define which marketing strategies are most effective during each phase.

As an entrepreneur, your time and money are limited. By thinking of the Key "A" Factors when creating your marketing plans, you'll be able to efficiently and effectively build strong relationships with your customers, and as a result, increase sales. It is the quality, durability and consistency of the three A's that will retain your customers in a lifelong relationship with your brand.

Once you understand where you are with each of your customers on the *Dating Lifecycle Curve*, you'll be able to apply marketing and branding strategies that will help you to acquire new customers and build long-term relationships with your existing customers. In the chapters that follow, I'll define workable strategies for your company if you're selling a product, and other strategies if you're selling a service. After reading this book, you'll be equipped with an array of new techniques that will help you better market your products and/or services to your target customers. As a result, you are certain to increase sales and take your business to new heights.

Chapter 3

Love at First Sight—
Presenting an Attractive Package

Every Friday, Sarah looked forward to happy hour with her friends at Rush Tavern in downtown Chicago, a favorite hangout of many young professionals. Sarah had recently broken up with her boyfriend of two years and was once again single. She wasn't really looking for a new relationship, but if one fell in her lap, she knew she would gladly take it.

At exactly 5:30 p.m., Sarah walked into Rush Tavern, and as she looked for her friends, she noticed a handsome man gazing in her direction. He was the definition of tall, dark and handsome, with crystal blue eyes, dark wavy hair, and biceps that could crack a walnut. The man smiled at her and slowly sauntered her way, looking as if he had just walked off the cover of GQ Magazine. Sarah's heart raced. She felt butterflies in her stomach. She turned to see if maybe he was walking over to meet someone else, but she realized that there wasn't anyone behind her. When she turned around again, he was standing directly in front of her.

"Hi, I'm Stephen," he said in a deep velvet voice, smiling and extending his hand. "Haven't we met before? You look very familiar." Not the most original line, but Sarah had heard far worse. They made small talk for a few minutes, then Stephen of-

fered to buy her a drink. Sarah graciously accepted and knew in an instant that she was head-over-heels for this confident, handsome man, and that there was no turning back.

*   *   *

Falling in love with brands is not so different from falling in love in real life. *Love at First Sight* is the consumer's very first experience with your brand, and it is driven primarily by physical desires of lust and attraction. We can all remember a time when we saw someone whose appearance caused us to have heart palpitations and feel as though we were falling in love. In terms of retail, many women can remember a time when they saw a pair of shoes or a purse that seemed to call out to them by name. Or a piece of jewelry that hypnotized them into not just wanting, but *needing* to have the item in their collection. In parallel, boys often grow up with posters of dream cars on their walls, and as adults, the mere glimpse of a sexy roadster can still cause them to fall in love. In today's marketplace, millions of messages compete for customers' attention. What this means is that the first thing a customer will notice about your brand is often your name and logo. It's imperative that your brand oozes sex appeal and creates desire and lust in the mind of your customer. In order to do this, you must focus on creating an attractive brand through your name, logo and color choices.

> **Love Note:** *Everything you create to represent your brand should stand out in a crowd.*

CREATING ATTRACTION FOR YOUR BRAND

The first step to developing attraction for your brand is to create a memorable brand image. Below are some key elements that should be considered as you build your brand.

1. Create a Captivating Name

Your company name is your calling card. When you're launching a new business, product or service, it's critical to create a name that is attractive to your target audience. A brand name should be short, memorable and have a distinctive sound and melody. Most business names are one or two words. For example: Starbucks, Nike, Macy's, Express, BMW, Mercedes, 7-Eleven, Jet Blue, etc.

So how do you create a memorable brand name? Start by brainstorming words that are related to your brand, as well as words that appeal to you, and write them down into two columns (see chart below). For example, the word "buzz" has a distinctive sound and could be a great name for a variety of businesses. Review the list to see if there are any stand-alone words that might work well for a brand name. Then start combining words to create a unique brand name. For example, if I were opening up a new swimwear boutique, my brainstorming might look like the list below:

Sunshine	Buzz
Swim	Eternal
Beach	Pink
Sand	Watermelon
Fun	Fish

The next step in the naming process is to determine if the brilliant brand name you've created is available. First, you'll need to search to see if the URL (website address) is available, because that is the first place many people now look for a company name. Go to any domain search website such as www.register.com or www.godaddy.com and type in your new name. Be sure to select the ".com" extension. If your name is available—great! Go ahead and buy it, along with the .net, .info, .org and any other extensions. Why do you need to buy the extensions? Because, for example, you could purchase www.eternalsunshine.com but not www.eternalsunshine.net, and a competitor could purchase the .net name and later steal business from you. This could be hazardous further down the road, because when someone searches for "Eternal Sunshine"—both URL's will be listed in search engine results.

WARNING: Many entrepreneurs are in love with their brand name and are disheartened when they see that the ".com" name is already taken, but elated when the .net extension is available. DO NOT DO THIS! You need to create an entirely unique name and purchase all the .com, .net, .biz, .org, etc. extensions associated with that name so no other business will purchase those related extensions. Remember that consumers will always go to the .com website address first, no matter how much money you spend advertising your .net extension.

2. Design a Seductive Logo

A logo may consist of only your brand name... but it may also contain an image. For example, Nike utilizes the "swoosh" to represent their brand, but their brand name "Nike" is also used consistently, and always in the same font. The Gap doesn't have any images attached to their logo, but the font used in "The Gap" is always consistent and never changes.

Your logo will be the very first thing that new customers see when being introduced to your brand. It must be attractive, and it must scream, "Pick me!" In order to achieve this, my advice is to hire a branding expert to create your logo. Graphic designers go to school to learn how to create logos that represent specific brands that stand out in a crowd. You don't need to spend a lot of money when creating a logo, but you do need to spend something.

I don't, however, recommend working with an ad agency. Their fees are often very high, and you can usually obtain a great logo elsewhere for a fraction of the price. Freelance graphic designers can be found online, at networking events, or through the recommendations of friends. Many times I've posted on my personal Facebook page that I'm looking for a graphic designer, and friends have quickly recommended some great suggestions. You can also find excellent graphic designers on many of the now-popular bidding websites, such as www.guru.com or www.elance.com. Or you could even hire a graphic design student by contacting local schools.

One of the most important things about your logo is your font choice. The font used in the brand name and logo should also reflect the mood of the brand you're trying to portray. Things such as luxury, whimsy, quality and other attributes can be (and are) conveyed through the selection of a font. For example, which brand name below seems to convey fun, fashion, and whimsy?

A.
Eternal Sunshine

B.
Eternal Sunshine

In my opinion, Choice A inspires a fun and whimsical feeling, while Choice B inspires a more serious and business like feel (thus making it less appropriate for the brand image we're trying to create).

> **Love Note:** *The design of your logo must be both attractive and memorable. Proper name and font selection will help create the mood of your brand and leave a positive impact in the consumer's mind.*

3. Color Me Beautiful

Your brand's color scheme is another critical decision when creating key elements such as your logo, signage, packaging, paint colors for a store, etc. Even as a small business, it's important to begin the branding process by choosing your corporate colors.

So... select two or three colors that will define your brand. And be consistent in your use of these colors! If you're using green as one of your colors, be sure to be consistent in the exact shade of green you use. There is a huge difference between a neon green and an olive green—each shade inspires completely different emotional responses in the consumer.

Your colors should be prominently displayed on your logo, business cards, website, social media pages, storefront, shopping bags, etc. And these colors *must* stay consistent throughout the lifetime of your brand. For example, Coca-Cola has consistently used red and white on their traditional cans and bottles, while Diet Coke stands alone because of the silver, red and black colors used to distinguish this secondary brand.

> **Love Note:** *Select two or three colors that represent your brand and use them consistently. Be sure to use these colors in all of your advertising pieces, including your logo, packaging, retail shopping bags, social media, website, advertisements, etc.*

How do you choose which colors work best for you? Some people may simply have a feeling about certain colors. Other entrepreneurs hire a graphic designer to select which colors to use when they first design their logo. If you understand the psychology of color, you can better attract new customers to try your brand. Remember: You only have three seconds to capture the attention of a new customer, so it's important that your logo stands out with both captivating design and color.

4. Establish Alluring Price Points

When establishing pricing during the *Love at First Sight* phase, it is imperative to set price points that will entice your target customer to try your brand for the first time. However, it's important to keep in mind that once a price point is established, it is very difficult for companies to raise prices in the future. Consumers will come to expect those initial prices, and they will even anticipate a "sale" price. But they will *never* expect or appreciate a price increase. This is one fundamental reason why new companies should never advertise "cheap" pricing during the *Love at First Sight* phase.

So... establish pricing that is appealing and that provides a sense of value and ownership in your consumers. If your brand is targeted toward the value-oriented customer, it is important for you to establish pricing that will sustain the operations of the brand in the long term.

By offering sales and other promotions, consumers will be drawn to your brand but will also have an awareness of the actual price of the brand. For example, if you launch a product or service with a very low price point as part of an initial trial offer, know that the low price point will likely become your customer's point of reference. However, if you want to offer a lower price in order to entice consumers to try your brand, consider offering a discount off the original price. For example, a hairstylist who offers "25% off a $100 haircut" to new customers will initially make $75... but the customer will know to expect the $100 price point in the future.

> **Love Note:** *Love at First Sight is the consumer's first experience with your brand. Price points need to be attractive and alluring, but not so low that you forgo profitability or tarnish your brand image.*

Whether you are selling value or luxury, it's important to establish a price zone for your brand during the launch phase. The **Price Zone** is the elasticity of price points that consumers will feel comfortable paying. It helps to calculate the highest and lowest prices that you'll charge for your brand. For any product or service, there is a "price ceiling," and once consumers reach this ceiling they will no longer go above it to purchase that brand. The opposite is also true: Once a brand is too cheap or becomes undervalued, consumers will almost certainly lose interest. Remember, it's much easier to lower prices than to raise them, and customers will always remember the starting price point.

LOVE AT FIRST SIGHT AND THE KEY "A" FACTORS

If you want your customer to fall in love at first sight, it is imperative that your brand is available to your target customer at the right place and at the right price. What's inside (Assets) will play a key role in later phases of the *Dating Lifecycle Curve.* But during the *Love at First Sight* phase, your brand must be physically alluring (Attraction) and available at the right place and the right price (Availability) in order for the consumer to decide to purchase your brand for the first time. "Love at First Sight" is all about seducing new customers to become interested in starting a relationship with your brand.

The Attraction Factor

It is critical that the external appearance of a brand is emotionally and visually appealing. You can utilize various means of promotion to seduce consumers, such as the design of your retail store, product packaging, advertisements, websites and social media platforms. It is also imperative that all vehicles chosen make the product/service stand out in a crowd.

Retail Stores

Any new retail store should be visually appealing to the target customer through the use of design and color. Paint colors on the inside should also complement the colors of your brand's logo, and they should evoke a mood that matches the feel of your brand. If you have a luxury store, for example, select colors that evoke a luxury feel, such as purple, crimson, and gold. If you're selling products to men, choose more traditionally masculine colors such as blue and green.

Merchandise displays should be synchronistic with your brand image. If you're selling budget clothing, plastic hangers work well. On the other hand, if you're selling high-end merchandise, you'll want to use quality wooden or metal hangers, along with merchandise racks that evoke a luxury feel.

Window displays should also be used as part of your over-all scheme to seduce new customers during the *Love at First Sight* phase. The colors of the displayed merchandise should be bright and attractive from both short and long distance. If you're using mannequins, they should be appropriate for your brand and visually appealing. Remember that your windows are your 24-hour salesperson, and they are a perfect opportunity to showcase your brand's attractiveness.

Product Packaging

The words *beautiful, handsome,* and *sexy* (or any other adjectives that might describe your customer's ideal mate) should also be used in your approach to packaging design. Product packaging is what the consumer sees after your brand name and logo. It should be visually appealing and employ the right colors, materials, graphics and copy. All the information shared above about designing your logo is also applicable to designing product packaging. Again, just like in the dating world, it is someone's external qualities, i.e., the way they look, that first attracts potential mates. In marketing, the goal is to seduce new customers.

When adding copy to your packaging, always remember that "less is more." The fewer words, the better. You have mere seconds to capture a consumer's attention. They will usually only read a few words that are in large print, so your wording should be as captivating as the images and colors on your packaging.

To create attractive packaging, I recommend hiring a packing designer or graphic designer who is professionally trained in this arena. If hiring someone is not in your budget, I recommend creating two or three different versions of your packaging to test. Test colors, images and copy before you choose your final package. *And don't just ask your friends what they think about your packaging!* Friends will almost always give you a biased answer. It is far better to ask people who could be your potential customers. You could hold a focus group, or you could post images of your package on social media sites and ask for feedback. You could also create a contest—"Vote for your favorite design!"—or even ask consumers to submit a design for your packaging. Facebook, Twitter, Instagram and Pinterest are all valid social media forums that promote sharing and are great platforms for customer participation.

Advertising

Seduction is not just about sex appeal in the *Love at First Sight* phase, but more about piquing curiosity about your brand among new customers. Advertisements should be sexy—but this does not mean that super-models should be used in every ad. Rather, beauty is in the eye of the beholder... or better yet, sexiness is in the eye of your target customer. The point is this: It's important to understand what your target customer finds attractive. If you're selling cookies, for example, mouthwatering photos of the cookies along with your brand's logo, colors, graphic design and slogans can all help to create a *Love at First Sight* response.

Money spent on ineffective advertising is money wasted, and even new companies should perform an annual audit to ensure they are producing materials that attract consumers on a *Love at First Sight* level.

A graphic designer will understand what it takes to create a *Love at First Sight* ad. However, if you are on a tight budget, you can contact local colleges to find a graphic design student ready and willing to work more cheaply. And again, you can post your advertising project on freelance bidding sites such as www.guru.com or www.elance.com. Even if you only have $50 to spend on creating an ad, you'll be amazed by the number of submissions you'll receive from around the world within hours.

Services

In order to make a "service" attractive, it must be (1) unique in some way and (2) wrapped in a pretty package. For example, there are millions of salons where women can get their hair cut. However, in order to attract customers, the exterior and interior of a new salon should be stunning. Therefore, your logo, signage, fixtures, paint colors, windows, etc. should all work together to create a gorgeous, seductive experience for your customers.

As stated above, ensure that your logo and brand name stand out from the competition. For example, if you're selling bicycle tours through the wine country, most of your potential customers will likely first learn about you through your website. Therefore, your website should have picturesque photos of the wine country, as well as a captivating brand name, logo and colors to peak a potential consumer's interest.

However you package your service—whether it's in a storefront or online—it's important that your presentation is absolute perfection, and that it creates feelings of lust and desire in your potential customers.

Websites & Social Media

We are all attracted to beautiful people, places and things, and your websites and social media platforms should be designed with this in mind. Your website should have beautiful images, engaging copy and an outstanding site design. It should be seductive, novel and captivating to your target customer. The colors of your website should match the colors of your logo and overall brand image. For example, if you visit www.Target.com, you will find that it is *always* red and white, matching the company's brand colors. The Target bulls-eye logo is prominent on their website, Facebook, Twitter and YouTube pages, which helps to reinforce the Target brand image.

You can design a website yourself, or hire a freelance web designer to do it for you. If you want to design it yourself, there are many terrific "design your own" resources that offer useful templates; you don't need to learn any complicated coding language. Simply select your design template, then add photos, text and navigation. WordPress also offers templates to create an attractive website or blog for your company.

If your website needs to be more in-depth, I recommend working with a professional website designer. You can find affordable freelance designers through websites such as such as www.elance.com, www.guru.com, or www.rentacoder.com. Be sure to check all potential freelancers' references and examples of their work. If you have a tight budget, consider bartering or trading products/services with a website designer—an approach that can make everyone happy.

The Availability Factor

Availability involves both the location and the pricing of a brand. In order to ensure that you are positioned to attain *"Love at First Sight,"* you must remember that location and appropriate price points will place you in front of new customers. At the beginning of your business or brand launch, it is vital to decide which customers you would like to target. This information is crucial in helping you decide where to advertise, where to sell your products, and how to set appropriate price points.

Retail Locations

Location, location, location! A retail establishment should be in the right location in order to attract the right customers. When researching locations, it's important to spend time at your desired location and watch customer traffic. Are certain days of the week busier than others? Will people be able to find you by walking or driving near your location?

Your retail location should be easy to find; consumers don't have time to go on an adventure to find a new location. They aren't lazy—they're busy. Like you, they are overwhelmed with countless "to do" lists and obligations. So, you have to help them fall in love with your brand by selecting a location that is convenient and accessible.

Consumers may also be drawn to your store by seductive pricing. And, of course, ensure that your price points enable you to make a profit. Determine if you want to draw the customers into your store with an attractive sale rack in the front of your store, or if you want to pull them all the way *through* your store by placing the sale merchandise in the back. Attractive and informative window signage may also be used to promote sales and other attractive pricing models that might appeal to new customers.

Product Placement

Products should be placed inside retail stores where your target customers can easily find them. Within a store, it's imperative to arrange products so that customers will see them and instantly fall in love.

Product marketers pay big money to be placed on end-of-aisle displays (**end caps**), cash register positions (**POS = Point of Sale**), and shelves at eye-level within grocery stores. If your company is producing products to be sold in retail stores, work with retailers to see if they have any special POS programs to position your product in advantageous locations in their stores. Some stores may charge a fee to locate your product on a certain shelf or near the cash register. In order to reduce this cost, you can offer the retailer incentives, such as a reduced rate, improved terms, or an agreement that you'll mention their store in your advertisements. Then, after placing your product, visit the stores or ask the retailer to take photos of your product's placement.

> **Love Note:** *If a new product or service looks good and is at the right place at the right time, customers will be easily swayed to try it.*

Advertising

It is important to create ads that will be seen by your target customers. Do your customers listen to the radio, watch television, read certain magazines, or use online websites? If you are selling running shoes, your customer may read running and health magazines both online and offline.

It's important to test your ads in different formats to see which one works better for your target customer. Understand which advertising vehicles are the best fit for your brand, and which are the ones used by your target customer.

Online advertising includes rotating ads on search engines, websites, or blogs. You can work with a company who specializes in online marketing, or contact websites directly. Most online companies have a media kit that explains their advertising rates, length of run, ad size and other information (such as the demographic data of their readers).

Facebook is another online advertising option that is gaining popularity. It is "smart marketing" because you, the entrepreneur, can determine who sees your ad by selecting specific demographic criteria. For example, an Atlanta-based purse company can easily create a Facebook ad that targets females between the ages of 25–40 who live in the state of Georgia.

The drawback to online advertising is that the response rate is often very low. But it's still a relatively cost-effective way to get your brand recognized by a large number of consumers.

Services

Companies that provide services may or may not have a brick-and-mortar location. If they do have a physical location, it should be located conveniently for their customers. Similar to retail stores, it's important to do a lot of research in order to find the perfect location for your business. For example, a fitness center should be in a location that is easy to find, has plenty of parking, and is close to their target customers.

If a company providing a service doesn't have a physical location but has an online presence, their marketing should ensure that the brand is at the forefront of the consumers' mind through an easy-to-find website, search engine optimization, and targeted advertising campaigns. For example, many people book travel through online websites such as Travelocity, Kayak and Expedia. These companies operate strictly online. In order to be "available" to their customers, they spend a lot of money on advertising in order to let their customers know that they are always there to meet their needs, 24 hours a day, simply by typing their names into a web browser.

Just as with product-oriented businesses, pricing for service-oriented businesses needs to be enticing in order to engage new customers. The service industry is very competitive; therefore, new service companies must offer attractive pricing options. And whether you're a luxury or value service brand, always ensure that your pricing strategies match your brand image.

Websites & Social Media

There are millions of websites and social media platforms that sell similar products or services. In order to stand out in the crowd, brands must ensure that customers can "find and follow" them very easily.

Your brand name should always be the name of your website, blog, Facebook, Twitter, Instagram, YouTube and Pinterest pages. Brand consistency is crucial across all online and social media platforms. When choosing a new name for a brand, it's not only important to see if the URL (web address) is available, but also if the name is available on Facebook, Twitter, YouTube, Pinterest, etc.

Imagine a new company called "Chic Frocs" that has just launched a line of sundresses. It's imperative that this company obtains the website, Facebook, Twitter and blog with the exact name "Chic Frocs," which should make it very easy for customers to find the brand across many social media platforms. Some customers may stumble upon your brand using Google search or after viewing an online advertisement. In order for your brand name to appear on the first page of search results, there are a variety of options to be considered. **Search**

Engine Optimization, or **SEO**, helps brands optimize their websites so that they'll appear higher on the results pages of major search engines, namely Google. You can also purchase key words through Google AdWords in order to help your brand appear on the first few pages. For example, if you are selling watches, you can purchase the word "watch" and each time someone types the word "watch" into a search engine, your website will appear higher in the results page.

The Assets Factor

The Assets of a brand are defined by the *internal* attributes and characteristics of that brand, such as taste, reliability and efficiency of service. Assets are not critical during the *Love at First Sight* phase, because the consumer has not yet experienced your brand. However, your brand's Assets will become the major factor in achieving the all-important customer retention, which will be covered in the next chapter, *The First Date*.

LOVE AT FIRST SIGHT TAKEAWAY

- The main focus of the *Love at First Sight* phase is to acquire new customers.
- Create an easy-to-remember brand name.
- Your brand's color scheme should be consistent over all of your marketing materials, including your logo, website, shopping bags, interior paint colors, etc.
- Everything you do in your business should focus on seducing new customers by conveying your brand's

attractiveness and availability. Think about the last time you saw someone who made your heart skip a beat — they were probably gorgeous and you were at the right place at the right time.

- Attraction and Availability are the two most important Key "A" Factors in the *Love at First Sight* phase.
- The interior and exterior design of a retail store must be attractive in order to capture new customers during the *Love at First Sight* phase.
- Products should leap off the shelves with exquisite packaging that attracts your target customer.
- Your website should be seductive, beautiful and captivating to your target customer. Remember, you have less than three seconds to attract the consumer and to seduce them into staying on your website.
- In order for the customer to fall in love with you, it's important to be available—at the right place, at the right time, and at the right price.
- Pricing must match consumer's expectations of your brand.

Chapter 4

The First Date—Making That
First Experience Count

Stephen and Sarah talked for hours the night they met at Rush Tavern. They exchanged phone numbers at the end of the evening, and Stephen promised to be in touch. After waiting the mandatory two days, Stephen called Sarah to invite her to dinner. Sarah, of course, was thrilled. She knew she was supposed to say that she was "busy" on Friday night, but she forgot all of the rules when she heard Stephen's deep voice on the phone. "Friday at 7 p.m. is perfect," she said excitedly. "I can't wait to see you."

Stephen arrived at Sarah's door with a bouquet of flowers and a bashful smile on his face, and he took Sarah to a quaint French restaurant for a candlelight dinner. It was the perfect place to talk and get to know each other. Sarah had always thought first dates were like job interviews—answering questions that could easily be covered by handing someone a printed resume. At this point in her life, Sarah felt like a professional interviewer; she had been on many first dates that had ended poorly and never morphed into a second date. Although first dates were not Sarah's favorite event, going out with Stephen was different. She wanted to know everything about him, and she was having so much fun that she hoped their date would never end.

*   *   *

Love at First Sight is governed by an emotional attraction to a brand. Generally, this attachment is based upon physical characteristics, since very little in-depth interaction with a brand has actually taken place. During this phase, it is primarily Attraction and Availability that capture the heart of the consumer. But the *First Date* phase is the moment when the consumer experiences a brand's Assets for the first time. It's the point where you, the entrepreneur, must make a favorable impression and seduce the customer to enter into a potential relationship.

It can be scary asking someone out for the first time. But if you have a good feeling about a person, and there seems to be an underlying attraction, common interests, etc., then it's a little easier to make that first leap. Perhaps you shared a long, magical gaze across the room, or perhaps the other person was very complimentary and attentive after striking up a conversation. These and other scenarios are the all-important intangibles that can lead to someone inviting you out on a first date.

It's important that the consumer feels comfortable trying your brand for the first time. They're already attracted to you, and they want to go on a date with you. Your job now is to encourage them to go out with you. There are several ways to do this: samples, trial-size products, coupons, discounts, test drives, etc. The *First Date* then allows the customer to taste, test drive, try-on and experience your brand for the first time. At this point, the external attractiveness of your brand is not nearly as important as the internal attributes of your offering. Your Assets must now seduce your new customers. And most importantly, the customer must have such an amazing experience during the *First Date* that they count the days until they can experience your brand again.

CREATING A GREAT FIRST DATE

Below are some tips to help get you ready for your first date with a new customer.

1. Establish The "DNA" of the Brand

The **DNA** of your brand can be defined as the key elements of your brand, and these key elements are the most important factors in creating the very essence of your brand. For example, the DNA of McDonald's could be "fast," "convenient" and "affordable." Everyone associates these key elements with McDonalds... and have for the lifetime of the brand.

In dating, you may (and probably should) have a list of the three most important factors when looking for a mate. For example, your top three deal-breakers may be "tall," "kind" and "funny." If you meet a great guy who is tall and kind, but who doesn't have a sense of humor, then you'll know to move to the next potential suitor, and to do so without regrets. This approach can also save you a lot of time and energy, because you'll only focus on dating people who meet those top three criteria.

To determine your brand's DNA, close your eyes and think about three words you'd most like to be associated with your brand. These words will help guide you in creating your products and services, as well as in marketing and advertising pieces, merchandise choices, service selections, packaging, etc.

2. Ask Your Consumers Out on a First Date

It's your job to ask consumers out on a date, and if you've worked hard during the *Love at First Sight* phase, then consumers will happily answer "Yes!"

There are several easy ways to entice consumers to go on a date with you:

Samples: Product sampling is a great way to introduce new customers to your product. Food companies often offer free samples to entice customers to try something new at a grocery store, bakery or coffee shop... with the goal of luring them back to buy again.

Trial-Size Products: Small, lower-priced (or even free) portions of certain products can essentially be a *First Date* for many consumers. Trial-size products encourage customers to try the brand with very little risk. Cosmetic and fragrance companies have utilized this strategy for years, and with great success. Consumers love anything for free; they are almost always ready and willing to try a sample of a new product.

Test Drive: Car dealerships offer free test-drives because they want the consumer to have an amazing first experience (though a high-pressure car seller can often ruin this experience for the customer). There are also luxury clothing and accessory rental companies where consumers can "rent" a purse or other high-end items before actually them.

New Customer Discounts: In today's marketplace, consumers love discounts, which are an excellent way to seduce new customers to try your brand. But remember, the discount you offer must be substantial in order to get customers in the door. A 10% discount rarely works, but a 15–30% discount is perfect for a first-time customer. But beware: A huge discount, such as a 50% discount, might open you up to consumers who are only after the cheaper price. That 50% discount will also be the price stuck in their minds if and when they consider doing business with you again.

3. Wow Them With A Memorable Experience

The most important factor during the *First Date* is to ensure that your customer has a great experience. Think about the best first dates in your romantic life. What made those experiences so memorable? Perhaps someone surprised you with flowers, or took you to a romantic restaurant. And that was only the start of the date. What might have really captivated you was your interaction with your suitor… the butterflies in your stomach and the fantasies about a future relationship. From that amazing first date onward, you were hooked on "love" like a drug.

To reproduce this feeling in sales and marketing, it's important to ensure that your customer has a more-than-memorable *First Date* experience with your brand. This starts the moment your customer walks through the door, and it continues through their first use of your brand. It's important to put your best foot forward at every touch-point with the consumer. And this begins with quality—both in products and in services. Every moment must exceed your customer's expectations.

> **Love Note:** *Create a memorable first date by seducing your customers with excellent products and services. Quality, reliability and 5-star customer service should all be part of your first date with new customers.*

THE FIRST DATE AND THE KEY "A" FACTORS

Although Attraction and Availability opened the door to new customers, the Assets of your brand are the most important Key "A" Factor in the *First Date* phase. Customers were mesmerized by the beauty of your brand, so they were easily swayed to make that first purchase. But the moment a customer tries your brand for the first time, the Assets of your brand must rise to the occasion and make a positive and lasting impression.

The Attraction Factor

Keep in mind that your brand must be very attractive during the *Love at First Sight* phase. By focusing on the visible elements of your brand—such as your logo, colors, design and packaging—you'll be able to entice customers to go on a *First Date* with your brand.

The Availability Factor

Availability was also crucial in the *Love at First Sight* phase. Pricing and location helped open the door to the *First Date,* but since the *First Date* is about the consumer's experience with your brand, Availability is not the primary focus in the phase. However, if all goes well on the *First Date*, Availability will again become important as the relationship develops.

The Assets Factor

A brand's Assets are the single most important Key "A" Factor in the *First Date* phase. Your customer's experience on the *First Date* will determine if they will want to move on to a relationship with your brand. So, as mentioned above, quality is paramount in this phase.

Retail Stores

In order to seduce new customers to shop at your store, you can incorporate new customer discounts and coupons, or you could offer free samples to get them in the door. But once they walk through the door, your job is to provide an experience that exceeds their expectations. Ensure that your merchandise, interior design, packaging and customer service matches your brand's DNA. It's important to select merchandise fixtures, tables, racks and hangers that not only match your brand image, but also work well to display the merchandise.

Your brand image should be reinforced throughout the entire shopping experience. Everything from the store layout to the fitting rooms should fall in harmony with your brand DNA. Retail store packaging (shopping bags, tissue paper and boxes) is also an opportunity to further market your brand. Many customers hold onto retail shopping bags, which then become an excellent opportunity for your brand name to be seen in different markets and locations.

Lastly, and perhaps most importantly, customer service is *vital* to the success of any retail store. Be sure to train your staff on proper greetings, sales techniques and etiquette to guarantee that customer service is a priority in your retail operation.

Love Note: *In order for your customer to have a great first date with your retail store, be sure to focus on how customer service, merchandise, interior design and shopping bags give your customer an amazing experience while also meeting your brand's DNA.*

Products

Once you've established the DNA of your brand, you must ensure that everything you sell meets those standards. When consumers pay a lot of money for a luxury purse, for example, they expect that it will be durable (and beautiful) for several years. On the other hand, consumers who buy a cheap purse aren't usually surprised when it falls apart after one season.

Of course, all consumers want to have the BMW experience at a McDonald's price point. If you are somehow able to offer your customers luxury products at inexpensive price points, you will have customers for a lifetime. However, you may not be able to make a profit with this model, though you may be able to price your products so that customers are content to pay a little more, because they realize they're getting quality.

If a customer purchases an expensive bikini and it falls apart after one wash, they will return it to the store and most likely not shop there again. Quality is extremely important to build a relationship with your customers. Ensure that you are doing thorough quality control to better assess durability and reliability for all of your products. Consumer's expectations are high and have little forgiveness when they first start dating a new brand. Quality products that match consumer's expectations will ensure your new customers will want a second date with your brand.

Advertising

Advertising is a convenient way to invite new customers on a date, and it's important that you create a **Call to Action** in all of your advertisements. A "call to action" is a marketing message that encourages customers to do things like:

- *Order today! Call 1-800-xxx-xxxx!*
- *Flash sale! Shop between 9 a.m.–noon and receive an extra 20% off.*
- *Save 25% off your first purchase. Offer ends (insert date).*

It's important that your advertisements contain both a call-to-action message and an expiration date. For example, if you offer a coupon—"New customers receive 30% off!"—they may not be in a hurry to use it. But let them know that the offer doesn't last forever, and they will feel compelled to shop sooner than later. "New customers receive 30% off! Offer valid until (insert date)."

Services

Whether you're a bookkeeper, accountant, hairstylist or fitness club owner, your customer will judge your service based on their experience. So it's important that you not only meet, but also exceed, your customer's expectations.

The *First Date* begins when you first meet potential customers. A warm smile and welcome greeting go a long way. Take a sincere interest in all of your customers, and you'll find that a first date will soon turn into a happy dating relationship.

Also, offering a free service or new customer discount are great ways to encourage customers to go on a first date. For example, a hair salon could offer a free "ten-minute scalp massage" with a first haircut. This service costs the salon very little time and money, and it will enhance the first date experience dramatically. You could also offer a discount coupon for new customers to try your service—such as "30% off for new customers"—or an introductory price for new customers.

Websites & Social Media

The first time a consumer interacts with your website or social media pages, they quickly form an opinion about the ease of use of these sites. Be sure that your website is easy to use by creating a simple navigation bar on the top or left side of your website. Also, too many companies cram too much information on their home pages, making it impossible for consumers to find anything.

In addition to providing easy navigation, it's also important to create a simple checkout process (if you're selling products online). A good rule of thumb is that the checkout process on your website should take no more than three steps.

> **Love Note:** *Your customer's first experience with your website will determine if they will stay long enough to entertain the idea of forming a relationship with you. Ensure that your homepage is memorable, that your website is easy to navigate, and that the checkout process takes no more than three steps.*

The same thing goes for your social media platforms. The first time a customer interacts with a brand's Facebook, Twitter, Instagram, Pinterest, blog, etc., they must have an amazing experience that compels them to return. Seduce them with great content, photos, behind-the-scenes information, special offers and exclusive promotions. There are literally millions of brands competing for limited consumer attention in the virtual marketplace, so think about how your brand can stand out from the others.

It's especially important to provide engaging content that is relevant to the consumer and that consistently offers value.

For example, Bebe shows photos of their latest collections and pictures from their exotic runway shows on their Facebook page. The company also provides tips on how to style and wear their clothes, such as ideas about which shoes and jewelry work with various outfits. In addition, they frequently run online contests that prompt fans to "like" pictures... and if a picture receives 5000 likes, then the customer receives a 20% discount code.

Another great aspect of websites and social media forums is that they provide you the opportunity to offer coupons, discounts, trial events and samples of your brand. You can work with "Deal of the Day" websites such as Groupon and Living Social to offer potential customers a discount to try your brand. This is a great opportunity to expose your brand to a broad array of potential customers who may have never heard of you. But be wary of customers who only use these sites because of the deep discounts... they might become a *One Night Stand* if you don't create a memorable experience that makes them forget that initial price.

THE FIRST DATE TAKEAWAY

- Invite potential customers on a *First Date* with new customer discounts, samples and trial-size products.
- Seduce your customers with a *First Date* experience that exceeds their expectations.
- The DNA of your brand are the key elements—or three words—that you use to describe your brand.
- Retailers must ensure that everything inside their

store meets the DNA of their brand and offers a memorable experience to the customer.

- Create a "call to action" on all of your advertisements, encouraging customers to take action and do something specific when they see your ad.

- Remember: Quality is of utmost importance on a first date.

- Assets are the most important Key "A" Factor during the *First Date* phase, because new customers are interacting with your brand for the first time.

- Seduction during the *First Date* happens through the quality, reliability and durability of your brand's Assets.

- Websites should be easy to navigate and have a simple checkout process.

- Offer valuable information to customers on social media sites that engage them to join and to start dating your brand.

Chapter 5

One-Night Stand—
Avoiding a Finite Phase of Use

After spending what seemed like endless hours lost in intense conversation during their first date, Sarah invited Stephen back to her place for a cup of coffee. But sparks were flying... and coffee was the last thing on both of their minds.

The next morning, Stephen left by 7:00 a.m., uttering those famous last words: "I'll call you."

Sarah thought the date had gone really well. She had a glow about her for the next few days, and she was excited to see Stephen again soon.

Unfortunately, Stephen didn't feel the same way. He never contacted Sarah, and Sarah spent the next few weeks analyzing what had gone wrong. She thought she'd been the perfect date, and she'd even allowed herself to fantasize about Stephen becoming her future husband. However, Stephen had decided halfway through the date that Sarah just wasn't relationship material. Unfortunately, he never shared this sentiment with Sarah, and he had no problem with a one-night stand.

*   *   *

Although simplistic, this story provides a foundation upon which to analyze a myriad of marketing opportunities. It's crucial to remember that a consumer's first experience with any brand will determine if he or she will form a long-term relationship with that brand, or simply have a *One-Night Stand*. This fork in the road is called the **Critical Point**.

A negative *First Date* with a brand will lead the consumer into the *One-Night Stand* phase. This is a disastrous, finite phase that must be avoided at all costs. To do this, it's important to focus on how your brand meets your customer's needs. Identifying the "needs and benefits" of your brand is essential in avoiding a *One-Night Stand*.

IDENTIFYING YOUR BRAND'S "NEEDS AND BENEFITS"

First, ask yourself a few questions about your brand:

- What does your brand do for your customers?
- How does it meet their needs?
- How does it solve their problems?

Next, identify the benefits of your brand: What unique benefits do your customers derive by having a relationship with your brand? For example, customers need a car to travel from point A to point B, but all cars on the market can provide this service. Luxury brands, however, offer further benefits such as leather seats, rearview cameras, superior handling, rear-seat televisions, etc. Customers don't necessarily "need" these extravagant features, but they help to solve some of their problems and make their lives simpler. Rearview cameras benefit customers by helping them see more clearly when backing into a tight parking space. And televisions in the back seat help busy parents settle down their kids in order to have a safer and more enjoyable car ride.

Once you've identified the needs that your brand meets for your customers, and the novel ways in which your brand might further benefit them, ensure that the quality of your brand exceeds their expectations. You should implement rigorous quality standards, and ensure that each and every aspect of your brand is put through a quality test. Quality also extends to customer service. For example, does everyone on your staff engage customers with excellence? Or are their gaps in your customer service? Again, it is important to ensure that your customer's experience exceeds their expectations.

> **Love Note:** *Understanding how your brand satisfies your customer's needs and solves their problems will help you exceed their expectations.*

Brands that fall into the *One-Night Stand* phase will not be in business for long. To avoid this, it's important to research and test your brand before rollout, and to continue testing throughout the lifetime of your brand. This affords you the opportunity to find out if there is anything wrong with the quality of the brand, and if so, to make changes quickly. You must ensure that your brand is perfect before you launch to a larger audience in order to avoid the *One-Night Stand.*

Price Your Brand Accordingly
Some brands fall into the *One-Night Stand* phase because they offer cheap prices while ignoring the quality of the brand.

If a product or service is cheap, many consumers will often try the product at least once. However, I caution entrepreneurs against using cheap pricing as their primary tactic in seducing new customers for a first date, unless the quality of the brand far exceeds expectations.

> **Love Note:** *Cheap pricing may indicate poor quality, causing customers to undervalue your brand and potentially resulting in a One-Night Stand.*

It is imperative that proper pricing is established at the launch phase of any brand. The price must be attractive enough to seduce consumers to make the first purchase, yet high enough to prevent buyers from feeling like they've purchased a cheap product. As mentioned earlier, the initial price at which the consumer purchases a brand will usually become the "price ceiling" for that brand. It has been proven that consumers hold an innate belief that prices should only decrease over time; thus, they are very resistant to price increases. There is an inherent consumer expectation that companies should only lower prices or offer discounts; customers never expect that the opening price of a brand will increase.

Offering a lower price point is a marketing strategy that is often utilized by marketers to entice consumers to try a product or service. However, if a product or service is priced too cheaply, the consumer might associate the brand with being "cheap" or "no good." The lower price point may entice consumers to try the brand again, but they will forever label the brand as cheap. More likely, the consumer will never purchase the brand again, except perhaps as a last resort if they don't have enough money to purchase their preferred brand, or if their preferred brand is out of stock.

In the dating scene, this is what happens when a *One-Night Stand* morphs into another kind of relationship — often referred to as a **Booty Call**. A Booty Call happens when consumers occasionally purchase a product because it is cheap, not because it is their first choice. Most business owners don't launch a business with the intent of becoming a Booty Call. Nevertheless, some entrepreneurs aim to offer the cheapest product or service in order to attract new customers. However, if the product or service is of poor quality or "cheap," they won't be in business for very long.

> **Love Note:** *Be wary about pricing your products too cheaply, or you may become a Booty Call. This happens when consumers occasionally purchase a product because it's cheap, not because it's their first choice.*

THE ONE-NIGHT STAND AND THE KEY "A" FACTORS

To help you avoid a *One-Night Stand*, let's explore how the three A's can help a brand move into the *Dating* phase. A brand's Assets are the most important key "A" factor in this phase, and they are often the cause of a *One-Night Stand*. Consumers might have a *One-Night Stand* with a product or service and move onto another brand if any Asset is lacking, whether it's in service, quality, reliability, durability or value. In order to avoid the *One-Night Stand* phase, it's imperative that brands ensure that their Assets support the Attraction and Availability that the consumer felt during the *Love at First Sight* phase.

The Attraction Factor

Attraction is a major reason why the consumer goes on a *First Date* with you brand. However, brands that offer Attraction without compelling Assets will usually not survive beyond the *One-Night Stand* phase. Though a brand may "look good," if the product or service does not fulfill a customer's needs, it will fail.

Have you ever purchased a product because it was attractive and inexpensive, but it didn't work after the first use? For example, you might have purchased a cheap t-shirt that fell apart the first time you washed it. And inexpensive technology products might be "appealing" because they are attractive and affordable, but the product itself is often unreliable.

While it is important to seduce the consumer during the *Love at First Sight* phase, some companies make the mistake of focusing on the external and ignoring the internal characteristics of a brand. You can avoid the *One-Night Stand* phase by ensuring that quality matches the Attraction of your brand. Be sure to research and test your brand before rollout by using surveys, focus groups and secret shoppers, and ensure that the internal Assets of your brand exceed your customer's expectations. Quality, taste, reliability and excellence need to be above par in order for your customers to begin dating you.

The Availability Factor

Availability in the *One-Night Stand* phase is important, but if your brand is "too available," consumers might then take you for granted and perhaps move on to date your competitors. Your brand can be "too available" if you offer cheap prices in order to attract new customers. Again, this can be dangerous because consumers will buy your brand based solely on price while still holding you to extremely high standards... and they will often be severely disappointed. You want to price your products and services so that you invite potential customers to go out with you, but you don't want to make yourself seem so cheap that your brand image is diluted.

The Assets Factor

> **Love Note:** *Brands that lure potential customers with cheap prices will fall into a One-Night Stand with their customers if they don't have the quality to support their brand.*

Assets are the core of any product or service and include a brand's service, quality, reliability, durability and value. Unfortunately, many brands end up in the *One-Night Stand* phase because Assets are overlooked. Lack of quality causes the consumer to label a brand as "cheap," thus relegating it into the *One-Night Stand* category.

Retail Stores

If you own a retail store, you must ensure that the products you sell exceed your customer's expectations. Be sure to do your research on the brands that you carry. Read customer reviews, and work with your vendors to secure a fair buy-back or markdown policy if the brand doesn't sell. Test all of your products yourself before you put them on the merchandise floor. Ensure that your merchandise is priced appropriately, and focus on the quality, value, service, durability and reliability of your products.

Customer service is a very important factor that many retailers overlook, and as a result, many of their customers become a *One-Night Stand*. To avoid this, hire secret shoppers to visit your store at various times and test your staff's congeniality, knowledge and efficiency. Train your staff in both your products and your customer service offerings. Every step in the sales process—from the greeting of the customer to the checkout process—must reflect excellence and professionalism.

Products

The quality of any product is paramount in avoiding a *One-Night Stand*. Test all of your products before you launch your brand. Ensure that they are priced appropriately so they invite the customer to go on a *First Date* and so that the customer doesn't place in your brand in the "cheap" category. Continue to focus on the quality, value, service, durability and reliability of your products. For example, if you are selling salsa, you should conduct taste tests before rolling out the product. Also test the jar to ensure that it's durable each time you use the salsa. If you are selling t-shirts, be sure to wash and wear the t-shirts many times to see how they perform. Understand how your products meet the needs of your customers, and use this information to make improvements to your product whenever necessary.

Advertising

It's important to deliver on your promises in order to avoid the *One-Night Stand*. If you offer a coupon or discount, make sure that it is honored. And always depict your brand accurately in advertisements. With today's technology, it's easy to make something look beautiful that is otherwise unsavory when viewed in real life. All of your branding should be beautiful, but it should also give an accurate representation of your brand. Also, test different forms of advertising—such as magazine ads, postcards, online ads, email blasts, etc.—to ascertain which ones will best represent your brand. It's important to select the right places to advertise in order to reach your target customers. If the local discount coupon book or online coupon websites offer you a great deal, but you're selling a luxury product, don't fall prey; it might dilute your brand image and bring around "discount divers" that are only interested in a *One-Night Stand*.

Services

Whether it's a product or service, it's important to focus on the quality, value, durability and reliability of your brand. Remember that your service starts the very first time you interact with a customer. When a customer walks into a restaurant, for example, it's the host or hostess who introduces the customer to the brand; restaurateurs must ensure that the host, waiting and cooking staff all provide their customers with an excellent experience on their *First Date*.

A *One-Night Stand* usually occurs in a service industry because something obvious went wrong. For example, if the chef prepared a great meal in a restaurant, but the waiter was rude, the customer might never return.

Utilize secret shoppers to better understand how your service meets the needs of your customers and helps them solve their problems. Ensure that both the quality and customer service aspect of your brand exceeds your customers' expectations. Train your employees to offer five-star customer service to each and every customer, regardless if it's their first or one-hundredth visit.

Websites & Social Media

Websites and mobile applications often fall into the *One-Night Stand* phase. With the introduction of mobile devices into the marketplace, consumers have a plethora of websites and apps, literally at their fingertips, that allow them to purchase any product.

In order for ecommerce and mobile shoppers to become loyal customers, they must have a great first experience with your website. If merchandise is misrepresented in terms of color, photographs or descriptions, customers will be disappointed when their package arrives. And if delivery is delayed or the package arrives damaged, the consumer will quickly move on to other dating opportunities.

Competition is fierce among companies with a social media presence. Customers have a plethora of choices of which social media platforms to engage in (Facebook, Twitter, Instagram, Pinterest, etc.) and which companies to follow. In order to avoid the *One-Night Stand*, it's important to offer engaging content that builds a relationship with new customers. This content needs to be updated frequently and consistently in order to keep customers coming back. Remember: Social media is all about building a relationship with your customers. Use this tool to further exceed your customer's expectations by providing educational information, coupons, discounts, promotions, contests and questionnaires that engage them in developing a relationship with your brand.

THE ONE-NIGHT STAND TAKEAWAY

- A *One-Night Stand* almost always occurs because the consumer had a bad experience with your brand.

- The *One-Night Stand* consumer hasn't invested any time in his or her relationship with your brand, and as a result doesn't have any loyalty.
- Quality, service and reliability are what consumers seek in a long-term relationship.
- Research and test your brand before it is launched in order to shore up any problems and to ensure that customers will be 100% satisfied.
- *One-Night Stands* can be avoided if marketers focus on the Assets by understanding how their brand meets their customer's needs and how it solves their problems. This Key "A" Factor is often neglected and, as a result, brands can fall into the *One-Night Stand* phase with their customers.
- Ensure that both the quality and customer service aspects of your brand exceed your customers' expectations. Seduce your customers beyond initial attraction by focusing on the seductive qualities of the Assets of your brand.
- A Booty Call will result if the consumer's experience on the first date barely meets their needs, and doesn't exceed their expectations.
- You never want your brand to be considered "cheap," because this will never lead to a long-term relationship.
- Companies must ensure that the information available on their websites is accurate and updated regularly.
- Social media platforms should offer engaging content that is updated frequently in order to keep customers coming back.

Chapter 6

Dating—Sharing Your Competitive Advantage

Tiffany and Michael met on a flight to Baltimore, where they both lived. They sat next to each other on the plane, and once they began talking, they realized that they both worked in the pharmaceutical industry and traveled extensively for their jobs. Neither had problems meeting people, but it was difficult finding a mate who met all their dating criteria. Since they both liked travel and worked in the same field, they found a lot to talk about. Michael asked Tiffany to dinner the following night at a quaint restaurant along the waterfront in downtown Baltimore, and Tiffany happily accepted.

Their first date was magical. Then, the following week, they had a successful second and third date. Michael felt it was all moving a little fast, and he was grateful that he had an out-of-town business trip the following week. He really enjoyed spending time with Tiffany, but he was not completely over his ex-girlfriend, whom he still saw once a week. Tiffany was definitely smitten with Michael, but she hadn't removed her profile from her online dating sites. She continued to meet potential suitors, just in case things with Michael didn't work out. After all, they had just started dating, and she knew they weren't exclusive yet.

*   *   *

How do people start dating? It's simple: If they enjoy the first few dates with someone, they will move into the *Dating* phase. This is the very early part of a relationship where each person is just getting to know the other and ascertaining if there is any relationship potential. During this phase, individuals may still be dating a few people at the same time.

For the entrepreneur, what's most important during this phase, is to encourage loyalty in your customers and to convince them to stop them dating the competition.

In the business world, if a consumer enjoys the *First Date* with your brand, then they will hopefully start dating you. But as illustrated in the *Dating Lifecycle Curve*, there is still a very limited amount of loyalty in the *Dating* phase. Customers have gone out on a few dates with your brand, but they are not yet in an exclusive relationship with you. If a consumer finds a new brand that better fulfills their wish list, they will happily switch brands and go on a date with a competitor. So it's your job to seduce your customer and to encourage them to start dating your brand exclusively!

UNDERSTANDING YOUR COMPETITIVE ADVANTAGE

The first step during the *Dating* phase is to understand your **Competitive Advantage**. Competitive advantage is defined as the features and benefits of your brand that makes you unique. These features are usually two or three of your strengths that set you apart from your competitors.

Love Note: *Identify your competitive advantage by analyzing two or three of your brand's strengths. These are the things that make you better than the competition. Then, use your competitive advantage in all of your advertising and sales strategies.*

For example, imagine that a new nail polish brand, named "Fierce," was recently launched in nail salons across the country. Fierce's strengths are the brand's unique neon colors and the "F" shaped bottle that stands out on the shelves. These attributes are unique and provide Fierce with a strong competitive advantage in the marketplace. They also seduced new customers during the *Love at First Sight* phase because the nail polish was readily available at nail salons across the country; Fierce was at the right place at the right time. However, at this point, Fierce's customers may still switch to other nail polish brands if they are looking for more traditional color options, which Fierce does not provide. But Fierce understands its position in the marketplace and focuses on its competitive advantage over other brands in order to attract and retain customers.

Sizing up the Competition

Since loyalty is just being established in the *Dating* phase, it's imperative that you, the entrepreneur, acknowledge that new consumers may still be dating several different brands. Therefore, loyalty can be easily disrupted. Your job (and the focus of all your efforts) should be to become the number one brand in the eyes of your customers.

In order to do this, it's important to conduct a **Competitive Analysis**. A competitive analysis compares your business offerings against the competition. Review at least three competitors and analyze their products, services, pricing, location, advertising, websites and social media programs. This information will help you to better understand your strengths, and will then help you promote your brand's unique competitive advantage to your customers.

Increasing Your Availability

Time is a currency that most people don't like to spend. In today's world, everyone leads busy lives, and convenience often prevails. Thus it is imperative that customers are able to purchase your brand in a variety of different places. With the advent of online tools—via mobile phones and social media platforms—convenience shopping is on the rise. Understand where and how your customers like to shop, and offer them convenient opportunities to purchase your brand. This will give you an enormous advantage over any competitors who aren't doing the same.

Focusing on Consistency

As customers continue to date your brand, encourage them to forget about the competition and enter into an exclusive relationship with you. Elements—such as your brand's quality, reliability and durability—should be consistent every time your customers go out on a date with your brand. Customer service also needs to be addressed with your staff in order to ensure that your customers consistently have an amazing experience. If even one of your employees is prone to being in a bad mood, it is important that they never take it out on your customers *in any way*, because this could lead to a very short-term relationship with many new customers.

Wooing Your Customers

To convince customers to become exclusive with you, show your interest in them through customer-appreciation programs. This helps to foster brand loyalty. For example, Michael could bring Tiffany flowers on their next date, and even order a bottle of champagne. She, in turn, could send him a handwritten thank you card.

To encourage brand loyalty during the *Dating* phase of marketing, here are a number of things you can offer:

- Coupons
- New customer discounts
- Membership programs with unique benefits
- Birthday and holiday cards
- Complimentary coffee, champagne or bottled water
- Fresh baked cookies
- Free shipping
- Free valet parking

> **Love Note:** *Implement customer appreciation programs so that customers will choose you over their other dating prospects.*

DATING AND THE KEY "A" FACTORS

It's important to implement customer appreciation programs so that customers will choose you over their other dating prospects. These will also need to be seductive to help to foster a more loyal relationship with your customers and help them to forget about the competition.

How can you do this? During the *Dating* phase, it's necessary that all three Key "A" Factors work in harmony to continue to entice consumers to purchase your brand.

The Attraction Factor

As mentioned above, the *Dating* phase is an excellent opportunity to conduct a competitive analysis to better understand what may attract customers to your competitors. Once that is understood, you can use the unique Attraction factors of your brand to promote your competitive advantage. Ensure that you are increasing desire in the hearts of your customers by identifying and playing to your strengths. The attractiveness of your brand should be a core strength that encourages people to date your brand over any other.

Retail Stores

A consistent and attractive presentation will help foster a relationship with your customers, as well as build brand loyalty. Since Attraction is one of your core strengths, it should show both internally and externally in your retail store. Externally, signage should be prominent and remain consistent with your brand identity (logo, colors, brand name, etc.). Internally, your store should be clean and properly merchandised so your customers have a pleasant experience each time they walk in the door. In clothing stores, fitting rooms should always be spotless and clothes should be immediately returned to their racks. The merchandise in your window displays should be eye-catching, swapped out regularly, and it should always be consistent with your brand image.

Conduct a competitive analysis to better understand both the external and internal strengths of your competition's stores.

This will help you to understand your competitive advantage and, subsequently, how to share it with your customers.

Products

In order to successfully navigate the *Dating* phase, product packaging needs to be attractive so that it stands out from your competitors. Thus, another component of your competitive analysis should be understanding the relative strengths of your brand's packaging. Do your colors, logo and name evoke feelings of lust and desire when set against the competition? Your brand should leap off the shelves and jump into the customer's arms each and every time they shop, and every aspect of your brand identity (your logo, colors and brand name) should be prominently displayed on all packaging. Also, be sure to view your product placement in comparison with the competition in retail locations that carry your brand.

> **Love Note:** *The Attraction Factor of your brand is a crucial component of your competitive advantage.*

Advertising

An attractive advertising program will help build a sense of loyalty in your customers. Whether you're utilizing emails, magazine ads, television commercials, online ads or direct mail, consumers will begin to identify emotionally with your brand's logo, corporate colors, sound icons, audio triggers, visual imagery, spokesmodels and any other promotional vehicles. Analyze your competitor's advertisements both online and offline. Ensure that your competitive advantage permeates all of your advertising, and that the attractiveness of your ads surpasses your competitors.

Services

Review your competition and look for ways to offer something unique to your customers. Typically mundane services—like housecleaning or plumbing—can be made "attractive" if you offer a wide variety of options to your consumers. A hair salon could offer their regular services such as cut, color and blow-dry, but also add unique services or create value-added packages. And as always, focus on your competitive advantage and ensure that your customers understand what value your services offer over the competition.

Everything that a customer sees that is related to your service—such as your storefront location, website, service menus, etc.—needs to be a stunning example of your brand identity. Your brand's logo and colors should be consistent and provide a springboard to separate you from the competition.

Websites & Social Media

Customers' options for shopping online are endless, so make sure that your competitive analysis helps you better understand your strengths and weaknesses in this arena. Your customers' experience online should be quick, simple and pleasurable. Images should quickly load on your website, and the checkout process should be easy to execute; online efficiency will give you a competitive advantage over many of your competitors.

But this alone is not enough. Your brand's logo and colors should be pervasive throughout your website. Images and text should be gorgeous and pristine. To rise above the competition and make your site more attractive, you could also create contests to engage your customers. For example, a company could encourage their customers to sign up for their email newsletter on their website by giving them a chance to win a $50 gift certificate.

Contests are also a great way to get your customers involved through social media. Some fashion companies encourage their customers to post photos of themselves wearing their brand's clothes on Facebook, Twitter or Pinterest, and the best photo wins a free item or shopping spree.

Be sure to take time and review your competitors' social media platforms. By understanding their online marketing strategy, you will further harness your own competitive advantage, which you will then be able to further promote online. The attractiveness of your brand on social media should showcase your logo, colors, images, promotions and the exclusive educational content you provide.

The Availability Factor

In order for the relationship with your customers to grow during the *Dating* phase, brands must be readily available to the consumer. During this phase, entrepreneurs need to understand where their customers shop and create multiple **Distribution Channels** in order to make their brand easily accessible. Distribution channels can be defined as any point-of-sale opportunity, including retail stores, outlet stores, ecommerce websites, iPhone apps, catalogs, infomercials, kiosks, selling opportunities through Facebook, eBay, trunk shows, art festivals, flea markets, and more.

Retail Stores

Availability is extremely important for retail stores. If a retail business has only one location, it is imperative that the store's hours are conducive to their target customer. That could mean working longer hours by opening earlier, staying open later, or working during holidays. In addition, a retail store may decide to open additional locations, launch an online store, or develop smart phone applications. It's imperative that you understand where and how your target customer likes to shop so that you select the appropriate distribution channels. This will help to seduce customers away from the competition because your availability fits their shopping needs.

Products

Your products should be available in multiple locations in order for your customer to easily find you, and expanding into multiple distribution channels can help increase your Availability. For small product brands, if you're selling through arts and crafts fairs, or flea markets, you can expand by also selling to boutiques or online. If you're already selling your product in retail stores, you should consider launching a simple ecommerce website.

Wholesaling is the selling of merchandise to a retailer or vendor who then marks up your product and sells it to the end consumer. Wholesaling is considered business-to-business selling, because you are simply selling your product in bulk to another business. The best ways to expand your wholesale channel is by hiring sales reps, selling online, or expanding the number of trade shows you attend.

Advertising

Advertising options should increase in the *Dating* phase. It's important to review where you are advertising, then expand into further options. For example, if you have placed an ad in a magazine and seen some success, perhaps try some additional magazines. Or, if you've tried advertising in a particular print magazine, try their online version. And if you're already advertising online, look into additional online advertising options such as:

- *Pay-per-click*—You pay each time a consumer clicks on your ad. Companies such as Google AdWords, Google AdSense and Yahoo Search Marketing offer this service.
- *Pay-per-impression*—You pay each time your banner ad "pops up" on a web page.
- *SEO*—Tactics used to increase the placement of your website in search engines, generally Google. Experts in this area can work on your website so that keywords, page titles and image descriptions boost your website higher in search engine rankings.
- *Sponsored search engine ads*—Pay to have your website appear in the top portion or "sponsored links" section of search engines such as Google, Bing and Yahoo.
- *Facebook ads*—These are the ads that appear on the right side of Facebook profile pages. You can select various demographic variables such as zip code, gender and age to decide exactly who will view your ad.
- *Blog ads*—These ads generally fall on the top or right side of a blog. The demographics of the readership of the blog should align with your target customer profile.

Services

If you offer a service, always ensure that your customers are able to reach you easily. The *Dating* phase is the point in time of the relationship where you should implement multiple distribution channels or additional locations. For example, a hair salon should have information available on their website, Facebook, Twitter, Instagram and Pinterest. They could also launch a mobile application that enables customers to book appointments in real time.

A freelance graphic designer can be hired to upgrade a service business's website with the goal of generating leads for new clients. There are websites such as www.elance.com or www.Guru.com where freelancers bid on various projects submitted by entrepreneurs. This is a great way both for freelancers to expand their Availability, and for entrepreneurs to locate freelancers for particular projects at a reasonable rate.

Websites & Social Media

Customers use home computers, laptops, smart phones and tablets to view your website. Be sure to review how your website looks on all of these communication vehicles. Depending upon how your website is designed, customers may see a different website on a home computer versus their smart phone. Sometimes images don't load properly and the navigation changes when moving from a tablet to a home computer. It's important that your website is easily available (and consistently designed) on all computerized communication platforms.

Cyberspace is a fast-moving and ever-changing environment. New modes of information dissemination and commerce channels are developed daily. You must decide which social media platforms are right for your business and your customers. Though it's very time consuming to keep up with every social media platform (Facebook, Twitter, blogs, Pinterest, Instagram, Foursquare, etc.), you must be available on at least two or more platforms so customers can easily find you.

You can link some of the social media websites together so that when you post something on your blog it also appears instantly on your Facebook and Twitter accounts. This is a great way to save time. However, it could also be detrimental to your brand if you have the same customer interacting with you on more than one social media site. Your content should be slightly different on each platform, so that if the same customer is engaging with you on multiple sites, the content will seem fresh, engaging and seductive.

The Assets Factor

Consistency of your Assets is very important during the *Dating* phase. Brands must offer consistent quality and service in order to form a long-term relationship with their customers. Once a customer becomes comfortable with a consistent experience from your brand, it's critical to make them forget about the competition.

Customer appreciation programs will strengthen your Assets and elevate your brand above the competition. Such programs could include free valet parking, complimentary beverages, discounts, free add-on services, and much more.

Retail Stores

Every time a customer shops at your retail store, they should have a consistent experience in terms of merchandise selection and customer service. Since they are likely to still be dating multiple brands during the *Dating* phase, the quality of your products and services must help you rise above the competition.

But this alone is not enough. In order to sway your customers to become more loyal to your brand, it's important to show your appreciation for their patronage. Ideas such as fresh baked cookies, complimentary coffee, free alterations, or free valet service show your customers that you care. After a customer shops with you for the first time, send them a coupon via email or snail mail with a discount off their next purchase. This works well to encourage them to return and shop again. However, it's a good idea to set a minimum amount that they must spend in order to utilize this discount, for example, "25% off your next purchase of $100 or more!" in order to maximize your profit.

Birthday cards are another great way to show your appreciation to your customers, and remember to include a "Thank You" coupon that will encourage them to shop again soon!

Products

The internal qualities of your product need to provide a consistent experience each time a customer uses your brand. Consistency in itself is seductive to maintain a relationship with your customers in the *Dating* phase. If you are selling cookies, for example, their freshness, quality and taste need to be consistent. Customer appreciation ideas for product-based companies could include free gifts, discounts or value-added information. Food product companies could give away free recipes that highlight a variety of ways to use their products, or they could offer a free gift with purchase, such as a cookie cutter or a packet of coffee.

During the *Dating* phase, some companies implement a "Buy 10 and receive one free"-style promotion. Or you could offer low-cost "prizes," like how cereal companies offer a free toy inside children's cereal boxes. McDonald's applied this idea by offering free toys with their Happy Meals.

So put on your thinking cap: Is there some sort of prize or promotion that you could offer your customers when they buy your products that will readily advance your business?

Services

Each time a customer goes on a date with your service, ensure that quality, durability and reliability are consistent. For example, whenever a customer gets their nails done at a nail salon, they expect the same level of quality and customer service. However, due to the fierce competition in the nail salon industry, and regardless of a consistent quality experience, customers may still visit different nail salons based on location or convenience. But imagine if a nail salon also offered a free glass of champagne or a 10-minute shoulder massage with each manicure/pedicure, those differentiating factors would entice more customers to visit or "date" that nail salon.

Since your customers probably have a plethora of service choices, it's your job to make them feel greatly appreciated for choosing you over the competition.

Websites & Social Media

Shopping experiences vary greatly online, so consistency is paramount during a customer's shopping experience on your website. Continue to improve the ease of their shopping experience so that it is quick and simple for them to shop online. Customer appreciation programs may also be implemented online by offering free shipping, samples and special online shopping discounts. And it's important to encourage customers to sign up for your email newsletter, so you can send them promotions and other special announcements electronically.

On social media platforms, content needs to be consistent, as well as provide value. If your content is compelling and seductive, consumers will return frequently and spend more time on your social media sites over other brands. You can implement customer appreciation programs through social media sites by offering coupons, discounts and free samples. But it's also important to offer valuable content along with promotions. Many companies make the mistake of only posting promotions, deals and discounts on Facebook and Twitter, rather than sharing compelling content that engages their customers. Be sure to offer a variety of content in order to entice your customers to exclusively date your brand.

THE DATING TAKEAWAY

- The *Dating* phase is all about acquisition—persuading new customers to become involved exclusively with your brand.
- The *Dating* phase is also the point where loyalty begins to increase, because a customer is spending more time with your brand and starting to build a relationship.
- Seduce your customers to date your brand by launching customer appreciation programs, such as complimentary coffee, fresh-baked cookies, free shipping and other concierge-type services. This

will help to differentiate you from the competition.

- Conduct a comprehensive competitive analysis to know your strengths and weaknesses relative to your competition. Using this analysis, promote your unique competitive advantage so your customers understand what makes you better than your competitors.
- All three Key "A" Factors need to work in harmony in the *Dating* phase in order for your customers to ignore the competition.
- Advertising options should expand in the *Dating* phase to include additional online and offline venues.
- Understand where and how your target customer likes to shop, and select the appropriate distribution channels.
- Each time a customer goes on a date with your product or service, ensure that quality, durability and reliability are consistent.
- Continue to improve your online shopping experience so that it is easy and fun for your customers to shop on your website.
- Create contests or offer compelling content and promotions on your social media platforms in order to give your brand an advantage over the competition.

Chapter 7

Introduction to Friends & Family— Spreading the Word

After two months of dating, Tiffany and Michael decided to date each other exclusively, and they began to refer to one another as "boyfriend and girlfriend." They grew closer and closer the more time they spent together. One day, Michael found that Tiffany's toothbrush, t-shirts and a few other personal items had moved into his house. This made him happy, because it signaled that they were moving into the long-term phase of their relationship.

It was early November when Michael invited Tiffany to spend Thanksgiving with him so that she could meet his close friends and family. Michael rarely introduced his girlfriends to his family; he had only done so once before. But Michael felt that his relationship with Tiffany was moving in the right direction, and he knew the time was right. He was beginning to feel a strong sense of loyalty to her, and he couldn't imagine life without her.

*   *   *

The *Introduction to Friends and Family* phase of the *Dating Lifecycle Curve* signifies the point at which time and loyalty begin to increase at the same rate. This is an exciting phase for the entrepreneur, because customers are so enthusiastic about their relationship with your brand that they want to tell the world.

The introduction of your brand to friends and family means that your customers have become your brand's champions. Think of them as your virtual sales force; they are so excited about your brand that they want to share it with everyone! This is known as **"Word of Mouth" Marketing**. "Word of mouth" is one of the strongest forms of marketing, because it means that a new brand is introduced via a referral from a happy, enthusiastic customer. They are conveying this message: "Try this brand because I use it and I've had a great experience!" Customers innately trust the recommendations of others, and customers who spread the word about your brand will give it amazing credibility.

> **Love Note:** *Think of your existing customers as your virtual sales force. It's critical that your customers have a positive experience 100% of the time so they will be encouraged to engage in "word of mouth" marketing for your brand.*

Businesses that establish a loyal customer base over time will reap incredible benefits from "word of mouth" marketing. But the challenge for entrepreneurs is that "word of mouth" marketing often takes a long time to establish. You have very little control over how long it takes, and over what customers specifically say about your brand. Though "word of mouth" can be a wonderful benefit to your marketing strategy, never rely on it as your sole marketing tool.

Think about the last time you ate at a great restaurant. How many people did you tell? Most of the time, people will share a positive experience with one or two people. These people may or may not try the restaurant, but since the referral came from a friend, there is a much greater likelihood that they will.

It's imperative to get your customers excited about your brand in the hope that they will share their experience with friends and family. The customer has, by this point, invested significant time in their relationship with your brand, thus some serious brand loyalty has been established. At this point, your brand is a reflection of their personal tastes and habits.

To build your virtual sales force, it's critical that your customers continue to have a positive experience 100% of the time. One bad experience can lead to disaster, because the customer will likely share this experience with their friends and families, too. In this way, "word of mouth" marketing can backfire. Think back to a time when you had a terrible meal at a restaurant, or perhaps got food poisoning. How many people did you tell? In general, when a customer has a bad experience, they will tell approximately ten people. Thus, it's imperative to continue to deliver exceptional quality and service *at all times* in order to avoid the potential negative repercussions associated with "word of mouth" marketing.

GETTING CUSTOMERS TO BE YOUR BRAND CHAMPIONS

So how do you get your customers to become your brand champions, and do it swiftly? How do you encourage them to seduce their friends and family to try your brand? Here are some creative marketing ideas to help your customers introduce your brand to their friends and family.

Refer-a-Friend Program

Refer-a-friend programs are a great way to motivate your customers to become brand champions. You could offer a free upgrade whenever a customer sends you referrals. Or you could extend an incentive, such as a discount or a free gift, to the referred customer when they first try your brand.

> **Love Note:** *Inspire customers to talk about your brand with refer-a-friend programs, where they are rewarded with discounts, free upgrades or other promotions.*

Friends and Family Discount

You can also use your employees as your brand champions by giving them coupons to distribute to their friends and family. Employees who are enthusiastic about your brand will want to share it with their loved ones, especially if it's an exclusive offer. Friends and family customers love special discounts, because they feel that they're part of an exclusive club.

Customer Reviews

Many online companies post customer reviews on their website and social media platforms, because they know people feel more comfortable buying a brand if someone else has recommended it. Clothing companies such as Old Navy post customer reviews on their website about all of their clothing; customers write about an item's fit, fabric and their overall satisfaction with the product. As an entrepreneur, you can implement this on your own website via a customer testimonials page, or you could enable customers to post on your social media sites.

> **Love Note:** *Encourage customers to write a review about your brand online and post it on your social media pages.*

SPREADING THE WORD WITH SOCIAL MEDIA

If your customers love your brand, they will be happy to tell their friends and family all about it. The beauty of online "word of mouth" marketing, or **Viral Marketing**, is that it moves at warp speed. Viral marketing entails individuals spreading the message of your brand at lightning speed, and effectively advertising your brand to a huge new group of potential customers.

Let's look at a few social media platforms and how viral marketing can work for your brand.

Facebook

One way to launch a viral marketing campaign for your brand is to entice your customers to "Like" your brand on Facebook. Once they do so, your brand will show under the "Likes" section of their Facebook page, and it will also appear on their newsfeed for all of their friends to see. This is a permanent endorsement of your brand by your current customers, and your brand will then be seen by all of their friends on Facebook.

Many entrepreneurs run contests to encourage customers to "Like" their Facebook page. Some contest ideas include:

- The first 100 people to "Like" our Facebook page will win a free prize or gift certificate.
- If we reach 500 "Likes" within one week, everyone will receive a discount or a free gift.
- "Like" our page and receive a free guide or 'how-to' video.
- "Like" our page and receive a 25% off coupon.

Twitter

Twitter is the definition of viral marketing. It provides a wonderful platform for sending short messages and updates to your customers, and once you (or one of your customers) send out a tweet, it goes instantly to all of your (or their) followers. If your tweets are interesting and engaging, they might then be "re-tweeted" by your followers, giving your brand the chance to "go viral."

Also available on Twitter is the opportunity to index your tweets along with similar topics by adding a "#" (hashtag) before certain significant keywords (ex., #lipstick, #greatdeals). This helps increase the visibility of your tweets to other people on Twitter.

Ensure that your tweets are engaging, conversational and educational in order to help spark viral marketing.

Pinterest

Pinterest is a fun platform that allows users to "pin" or paste photos that they find interesting. It is also a great tool for entrepreneurs to organize photos, inspirations and ideas, and to share them with their customers. If one of your followers likes one of your photos, they can "re-pin" it to their board, so that all of their followers will see it as well.

You can start a Pinterest board for your business, and even create different boards that may or may not be directly affiliated with your brand. For example, if you own a shoe boutique, you can create a board with photos of your products, but also create additional boards that may be interesting to your target customer, such as boards focused on business, travel, dining, etc. This will help increase traffic to your brand by providing fun, seductive and unique content for potential customers.

Blogs

Another great way to commence viral marketing is to encourage bloggers to become your brand champions. You can do this by simply sending them information and a sample of your brand. For example, if you are selling artisan bread, send a free loaf to a successful blogger, along with information about your brand, including the history of your company and how your brand is different. If a blogger likes your bread, they may write about it on their blog, which will then be seen by all of their followers. Bloggers also have Facebook and Twitter pages where they share information about their blog posts.

Established bloggers have large, loyal followings. For example, "Purse Blog" posts reviews of different brands of purses, and it reaches thousands of potential customers every day. "Purse Blog" readers consider its posts to be endorsements of particular brands, and they are thus more likely to purchase that brand in the future.

Foursquare

You can use Foursquare as a viral marketing tool by encouraging your customers to "check in" at your location (if you have a brick-and-mortar enterprise). Each time a customer "checks in," it is shared with all of his or her Foursquare friends. For example, if John "checks in" at Rome Pizza every Friday night, his friends and family will assume that the restaurant serves excellent pizza. Business owners can also offer promotions, coupons and discounts to customers who "check in" frequently to their location.

FRIENDS AND FAMILY INTRODUCTIONS AND THE KEY "A" FACTORS

Attraction is the primary Key "A" Factor during the *Introduction to Friends and Family* phase. In particular, the attractiveness of your referral programs will encourage "word of mouth" marketing by increasing the loyalty of existing customers, and thus acquiring new customers.

Since your loyal customers are now telling their friends and family exactly where to buy your brand, Availability needs to remain consistent, but it is not a significant focus during this phase. Similarly, the quality of your Assets must continue to "wow" your existing customers, as well as their friends and family. But without an attractive referral program, the *Introduction to Friends and Family* phase may not occur at all.

The Attraction Factor

During this phase, potential customers are being introduced to your brand via brand champions. Thus your brand needs to be very attractive, because basically, you are once again being placed in the *Love at First Sight* phase. In some ways, this is similar to a blind date; friends are recommending you as a date to someone else, but at first, you be will judged almost solely on your looks. So it's important to utilize attractive referral programs in order to seduce both existing customers and their friends and family to become more involved in their relationship with your brand.

Retail Stores

In order to encourage your existing customers to share their love of your brand, you can implement seductive referral programs. These work especially well in retail settings. For example, you could offer a $50 gift certificate if a customer refers a friend. Or you could offer them 30% off their next purchase the next time they bring a friend into your shop. And in order to "convert" the referred friends and family to new loyal customers, you could offer them a 25% off coupon as well. It's a win-win for everyone.

Employees can also be part of your virtual sales team. Use them to spread the word about your retail store by allowing them to share a special discount with their friends and family. They can post this information on their Facebook pages, or pass out postcards with the information. Another idea is to create a special day for friends and family discounts. For example, on the last Wednesday of each month, friends and family could receive an additional 30% off their purchases. Pick the slowest day of the month to implement this program in order to increase your monthly sales.

Products

As a product producer, it's your job to be vigilant about the attractiveness of your brand. Current customers who recommend your products to their friends and family already think very highly of your brand, and they are ready to affirm their loyalty. You can implement referral programs that encourage customers to buy several of your products and share them with friends. Mary Kay encourages their customers to host parties where they invite their friends and family to purchase cosmetics, and the hostess of the party receives free gifts based on the amount sold.

If you have employees working on the manufacturing or marketing of your products, you could encourage them to get more involved by creating an "employee of the month" contest. The winner of this contest will receive a gift certificate and their photo on your brand's website. This will engage them to refer your products to their friends and family, as well as to share your website address.

Advertising

Incorporate "refer-a-friend" discounts into some of your advertising. For example, you could send a postcard or email to existing customers that offers them 25% off whenever they refer a friend.

Another idea is to utilize local celebrities to endorse your brand. In our society, many people look up to celebrities and often buy the brands that they are recommending. A national celebrity is usually too expensive for a small business, but perhaps there is a local celebrity that appeals to your target market and who would endorse your brand. You could feature this celebrity endorsing your brand on postcards, brochures, emails, magazine ads, online advertisements, social media and websites.

Services

Service businesses thrive on referrals from their existing clients. Since you are selling a service rather than a product, your customers will rate you based on your expertise in your field and their experience working with you. If your current customers love your service, they will want to share it with their loved ones.

The refer-a-friend program works very well for service businesses as well. The referral program needs to be attractive to both existing clientele and prospective clients. For example, a masseuse could offer a refer-a-friend program where referred customers receive 20% off their first massage. And existing customers who refer five friends could receive a free one-hour session.

Service businesses should also use their employees to help grow their business. You can implement a "friends and family" discount that your employees can offer to prospective customers. Print business cards for each of your employees with a "friends and family" discount on the back of the card, and give a bonus to the employee who has the most referrals each month as a motivator for them to promote your business further.

Websites & Social Media

Your loyal customers will convey their love for your brand with their friends and family by sharing links, liking photos, reposting tweets, or repining photos.

Retailers such as Bebe use viral marketing online to increase sales. If you shop on www.bebe.com and find a product that appeals to you, then click the "Like" button next to that product, and you can share your affection for that product with your friends via Facebook or Twitter. This is a very effective means of promoting both brand and a specific product, because it comes directly from a friend. You can implement this same strategy on your website by including a "Like On Facebook" button next to each of your product photos. If a customer "likes" your product, it will post on their Facebook page for all of their friends and family to see.

Customer testimonials may also be used on your website, social media platforms, packaging and in any other place new customers might have interactions with your brand, because people love to see what others are saying about products and services. People feel comfortable buying products/services based upon recommendations of other people; even if they are strangers. Therefore, customer testimonials can be used as a mechanism to seduce new customers to try your brand.

The Availability Factor

As always, your brand needs to be easily accessible, so that potential customers (in this case, friends and family) can easily find it. But because your original customers are telling their friends and family where to buy your brand, Availability is not a major focus at this point in the *Dating Lifecycle Curve*. However, it's still important to offer multiple distribution channels so that existing customers, as well as their friends and family, can easily find you. Price points also need to be "available" (i.e., within a comfortable range) in order to continue to strengthen your relationship with existing customers, while also appealing to new referrals. And it's advisable at this stage to keep pricing consistent and not make drastic changes.

The Assets Factor

The internal attributes of your brand must continue to "wow" your current customers, while also appealing to a group of new customers. A referred customer's first experience with your brand will determine if they, too, will pursue a relationship with you. So it's necessary to always focus on the internal qualities of your brand to ensure that your customer base continues to expand. However, when new customers are introduced to your brand in the *Introduction to Friends and Family* phase, it's similar to the *First Date* phase where they are meeting your brand for the first time and haven't yet experienced the internal assets of the brand.

THE INTRODUCTION TO FRIENDS & FAMILY TAKEAWAY

- In the *Introduction to Friends and Family* phase, loyal consumers who feel a strong emotional connection to your brand will want to share it with their friends and family.
- "Word of mouth" is one of the strongest forms of marketing, because it means a brand is introduced to new customers via a referral from an already happy customer.
- Businesses should never underestimate the power of referrals.
- *Attraction* is the Key "A" Factor in this stage due to the importance of attracting new customers through valuable referral programs.
- Encourage your customers and employees to "seduce" their friends and family to try your brand by offering them attractive "refer-a-friend" promotions, discounts and employee "friends and family" events.
- People are encouraged to try your brand when they see that other people are having a positive experience.
- Post customer testimonials on your website, social media platforms, packaging and any other place new customers might have interaction with your brand.
- Enable customers to post their reviews of your brand online. This will help them feel more involved with your brand and ultimately strengthen

your relationship with them.

- People are much more comfortable working with services that are referred to them by a friend or family member.
- Social media platforms enable individuals to spread the message about your brand to a new group of potential customers, via viral marketing.
- Contests are a wonderful way to encourage customers to "Like" your brand on Facebook.

Chapter 8

Engagement—Securing Customer Commitment

At Christmas time, it was Michael's turn to meet Tiffany's family in New York City. Michael couldn't believe his luck that they would be in Manhattan for the holidays. Ever since he was young, Michael had dreamed of proposing to his future wife on the top floor of the Empire State Building, at midnight on New Year's Eve. Reservations were hard to get, but he managed to reserve a table at one of the nicest restaurants in Manhattan. After dinner, he told Tiffany he wanted to watch the fireworks from the top of the Empire State Building. One minute before the stroke of midnight, Michael sank down on one knee and proposed. Before Tiffany could say anything, fireworks began erupting in the background. Michael couldn't have planned it any better if he tried.

Tiffany was surprised and delighted by the proposal. Moreover, she was flabbergasted by the size of the ring. She had always dreamed of a circular diamond surrounded with pave diamonds on a Tiffany setting. Michael had exceeded all of her expectations. They were a perfect match, with the same dreams and aspirations. After a year of courtship, she knew that Michael was the one. She couldn't wait to start planning the wedding, and to spend the rest of her life with him.

*   *   *

In marketing, engagement happens when customers have invested a significant amount of time in their relationship with a particular brand, and they are ready to commit. This is also the point on the *Dating Lifecycle Curve* that customer retention truly begins. Customers have invested in your brand and they have shown their commitment to you by the frequency of their purchasing behaviors. Their loyalty is very strong, which can and should be rewarded with some sort of loyalty program (which acts as an engagement ring). Once a customer becomes "engaged" to a brand, competitors all but disappear.

In dating, once a couple becomes engaged, they stop actively pursuing relationships with other people. However, the strength of the relationship may still be a bit uncertain, because they are not officially married and so still have the ability to leave the relationship without a lengthy or expensive divorce.

In marketing, it's less expensive to retain customers than it is to acquire new ones. Your existing customers already know you, and they have a strong desire to continue their relationship with you, whereas new customers need a lot of seducing, which costs a lot of money in advertising. Existing customers have fallen in love with you by the *Engagement* phase and will happily show their commitment to you over your competitors. A loyalty program is an excellent tool to retain your best customers, because it makes them feel "special" and part of a club. Customers invest their time and money with your brand, and they appreciate you showing them gratitude through upgrades, discounts, free gifts or other recognition tools.

> **Love Note:** *It's more expensive to acquire new customers than to focus marketing efforts on existing customers. Your loyal customers already love your brand and are happy to continue their relationship with you.*

SETTING UP A LOYALTY PROGRAM

To show your commitment to your existing customers, it's critical to utilize some form of an "engagement ring." Loyalty programs are important for several reasons. First, they encourage repeat business. Consumers have many choices today, and a loyalty program encourages them to continue choosing your brand over the competition. At this stage of the *Dating Lifecycle Curve*, your customers have proven that they have a very strong desire to continue their relationship with you, and a loyalty program helps to formalize that relationship.

Second, a loyalty program is low-cost advertising. Your brand name may simply be on a loyalty card that is always in your customer's wallet, which will help keep your brand at the top of their mind. And emailing customers who have enrolled in your loyalty program will create a consistent form of communication between you and them. Each time your customer hears your name, they will be reminded of your brand and of the many benefits you bestow upon them. The next time they're faced with the temptation to visit a competitor, they will stop and remember your loyalty program, and thus their engagement to your brand.

Airlines and hotels have some of the most popular and successful loyalty programs. Airlines use "frequent flyer miles" to entice consumers to fly repeatedly with their brand. Consumers have many choices of airlines when booking a flight reservation, but they will usually continue to purchase tickets with a particular airline in the hope of accruing enough miles to obtain a free ticket.

Five-star hotels offer loyalty programs where returning guests can receive free upgrades, such as better rooms, discount spa services, and exclusive dining opportunities. Many hotels also use a points program where patrons accrue points each time they stay in that hotel. With so many competitors in the hotel industry, customers will opt to stay with the hotel that carries their points in order to amass enough points (eventually) for a free stay.

Entrepreneurs juggle many things on a daily basis, and keeping track of points for a loyalty program can be very time consuming. Though loyalty programs don't have to be as intricate as a card or points program, it *is* important to keep sales data for all of your customers. For example, a small boutique could keep sales records for each customer, so they know how much they spend annually. This provides excellent background information for your loyalty program and enables you to focus your attention on customer retention.

It has been said that 80% of your sales is generated from 20% of your customers. So be sure that you focus on that 20%! If you have an online store, it's very easy to keep track of this kind of data. If you have a retail store, product, or service business, you can set up a simple system to keep track of your sales data. This means you could easily implement a loyalty program to focus on your best customers. Keeping track of this data will also help you better understand the demographics and psychographics of your customers.

Love Note: *Create a loyalty program that is simple to implement and manage.*

There are a few key things to remember when setting up a loyalty program during the *Engagement* phase:

1. *Exclusivity:* If you have a luxury brand, you may benefit from creating a loyalty program that is exclusive to your very best customers. This will make them feel as if they are part of an elite club (which, of course, they are!). You could also create a loyalty program that is "by invitation only" and that is based on their shopping frequency or sales volume.

2. *Set Limits:* Place an expiration date on your loyalty program in order to encourage customers to shop sooner rather than later. Customers will only reap the benefits of the rewards program by using it *before* the expiration date, which provides another opportunity for you to increase sales. You can also refresh the loyalty program each year in such a way that your customers' loyalty points start anew.

3. *Communicate:* Send out regular emails with updates about your loyalty program, and create special programs, engaging content, new products and incentives for your most loyal customers. Couples engaged in romantic relationships enjoy consistent communication, and it's important to follow this concept in marketing your business. However, be sure to send emails only once or twice per month. If you overload your customer's inboxes by send-

ing emails every day, they will quickly lose interest and your emails will no longer seem special. (Just think about the boyfriend who overly pursues a woman... she will quickly tire of him and move onto someone else.)

4. *Opt-in:* If exclusivity is not your concern, an opt-in program will enable more people to join your loyalty program. You can create a place on your website, emails or social media platforms that enables your customers to opt into your loyalty program.

5. *Simplicity:* However you decide to set up your loyalty program, keep it simple. There are affordable software programs that help you keep track of sales and points for your loyalty program. And always be sure that customers are apprised of their loyalty club status. If they know that they only need two more purchases to receive a free gift or discount, they will be more motivated to shop soon in order to achieve their reward.

6. *Seduction:* Ensure that your loyalty program is enticing enough that your customers will want to join and help them forget about the competition. Understand what motivates your customers (ex., free gifts, discounts, upgrades, etc.) to create a successful and seductive loyalty program.

Loyalty Program Ideas

So where do you begin? As mentioned earlier, your loyalty program should be simple and easy to implement, while also being attractive to your most loyal customers. You want to create an "engagement ring" that is so beautiful that your customers will totally forget about your competition.

Below are a few loyalty program ideas that you could implement for your business.

Loyalty Cards

You can create a simple loyalty program where the more your customer shops, the more benefits they receive. For example, a car wash could offer a loyalty card where with every ten car washes, the next one is free. Or a bakery could offer a free cookie for every dozen cookies purchased.

Tier System

Creating a tier system will motivate and seduce your customers to spend more money and increase their loyalty. For example, if a customer spends $1000, they will become a bronze member and will receive a $100 gift certificate. Then, if they spend $5000, they will become a silver member and receive a $500 gift certificate, as well as some other complimentary gift or service. And if they spend $10,000 or more, they'll receive a $1000 gift certificate and a free concierge service. American Express, for example, offers various rewards and incentives with their different levels of credit cards. Maybe you can apply this same philosophy to your business.

Accrue Points

Many companies formulate a loyalty program based on points such as: "accumulate 100 points and receive a free gift!" The more points a customer accrues, the better the gifts. For example, Sephora uses a basic points system: Every time a customer shops at Sephora, their dollar amount is converted into points. Then, at various point levels, Sephora gives away free beauty gifts. This is a time-consuming process, and it must be automated to be effective... but the results to your bottom line could be astounding.

Exclusive Shopping Events

Many retail stores offer exclusive shopping events to their best customers. Perhaps a store can open for special shopping hours, or host a cocktail party to introduce new merchandise. **Trunk shows** are special events in retail stores where a designer visits the store to introduce their latest collection. These can be special events for your very best customers. Trunk shows are seductive because of their unique nature and exclusivity.

Personal Shopper

Many people don't like to shop, and they are happy to accept the assistance of a personal shopper. Personal shoppers can help select gifts, coordinate outfits, alert customers to new merchandise, and style their customers for special events. If you are the owner of a small clothing boutique, you don't have to hire separate personal shoppers. Instead, you could train your current employees to provide these services to your best customers.

Concierge Service

You want to treat your best customers with a white glove service. For example, customers who spend $5000 or more per year could be entitled to concierge services, such as complimentary dry cleaning, restaurant gift certificates, valet parking, theater tickets or catered events. By knowing your most valued customers and what motivates them, you can create concierge services that will exceed their expectations.

Monthly Clubs

Another option is to offer your customers a monthly club program, which is a great way to generate guaranteed income as well as promote customer loyalty. If you're selling wine, for example, customers could sign up for a 3, 6, 9 or 12-month "Wine Of The Month" club. Customers pay in advance, and a different bottle of wine is mailed to them each month.

Membership

You could also implement a subscription service where customers purchase an annual membership. For example, it's much less expensive to join a fitness club if you pay for a year in advance instead of paying on a monthly basis.

Free Upgrades

Upgrades are an excellent way to provide exemplary customer service and make customers feel enthusiastic about their relationship with you. But the upgrades must be compelling, so that the customer won't later switch to another brand. For example, a hotel may offer a nicer room with a better view to a loyal, repeat customer, making it an easy choice for them not to pick a competing hotel right down the street.

Free Gift-Wrapping

This is a nice, low-cost service to offer all of your customers around the holidays, but you could also offer free gift-wrapping all year to your best customers.

Birthday Gifts or Discounts

Birthday cards, emails, discounts and gifts are inexpensive ways to recognize your customers and celebrate their birthday.

Customers want to feel appreciated, and this is a very simple and fun way to increase retention.

Gift Reminder Service

In today's busy world, it's hard to keep up with birthdays, anniversaries and other special events. A gift reminder service is an excellent way to help secure retention. If a customer stores all of their birthday, anniversary and other important dates with your company, they will develop a comfort level with you and rely on you to help with their gift-giving throughout the year. For example, some florists ask their patrons to share birthdays and anniversaries, which benefits busy professionals who don't want to forget special occasions. The florist's gift reminder service then alerts customers of these events, thus providing them with an effortless shopping experience. This experience could be even extended to mobile applications, where customers could be reminded, make a purchase, and pay for products via a mobile device.

Appointment Reminders

Service industries can send out reminders to their clients about upcoming appointments that they should schedule. For example, dentists often send a reminder card to patients about an upcoming cleaning appointment. And a hair salon could send an email telling a regular customer that it's time to schedule a haircut or color. Whichever loyalty program you choose, be sure that it works for you financially. Do you need to purchase new software or hire a programmer to set up a new system on your website? Analyze the costs of the rewards and how these fit into your bottom line. Be sure that whichever loyalty program you implement, you are (1) making money and (2) that your customers feel they are also benefitting. En-

sure you have room in your margins to give away a discount—
you don't want to be *too* generous.

> **Love Note:** *Whichever loyalty program you choose,*
> *ensure that it's profitable for your company.*

ENGAGEMENT AND THE KEY "A" FACTORS

Attraction is the most important Key "A" Factor in the *Engagement*
phase, because the attractiveness of your loyalty program is what
will motivate your customer to become engaged to your brand. All
three "A's" are important in this phase, because they continue to increase the loyalty of your customer... but the attractiveness of your
loyalty program is of the utmost importance. Keep in mind that
your work as a seductor/seductress is never done. It's necessary to
continue to "seduce" your customers throughout the *Engagement*
phase so they forget about the competition and focus solely on your
brand.

The Attraction Factor

Attraction needs to remain strong at the *Engagement* phase.
A brand must always attract target customers through appealing
design and marketing programs. The core elements of your brand
image (logo, corporate colors, package design, etc.) need to remain
consistent in order for even your loyal customers to easily identify
and emotionally connect with your brand. Because the customer is
not yet "married" to your brand, they could still leave if they find
another brand that is more attractive. Even though they aren't actively looking for alternate brands, there's still a chance that they
could leave the relationship.

Loyalty programs must also be attractive and seductive to the customer by providing enticing rewards. Customers must be excited to join a loyalty program because they can't wait to receive the program's benefits. A great loyalty program will make consumers forget about the dollar amount they are spending... all they'll be focused on are the rewards they hope to receive.

Retail Stores

Developing a loyalty program for your retail store is a great way to encourage your customers to shop more often and, as a result, to increase sales. You can create a tiered loyalty program based on sales volume. For example, if you own a small boutique, once a customer spends $1000 or more per year, they could be enrolled in the *Gold* loyalty program and receive 15% off on all purchases, as well as free gift wrapping. If they spend $5000 or more per year, they could be enrolled in the *Platinum* loyalty program and receive 20% off and free alterations.

Exclusive shopping events (such as a trunk show) work very well in the retail environment; they are a great way to showcase new merchandise and can be a lot of fun for your most loyal customers. Trunk shows give customers the opportunity to meet a designer and get a sneak peak at their latest collection. Many retail stores will offer wine, champagne and appetizers at these shows to make them even more festive, and to create a seductive and unforgettable shopping experience.

Product

Product companies can implement a loyalty program by offering a loyalty card. For example, a bagel shop could offer a "Buy 12 Get One Free" program. Coffee shops could offer a similar program: "Buy 10 coffees and get the next one free!" Rather than keeping points, you can create basic "punch cards" to keep track of purchases. This may seem old-fashioned, but if you don't have the ability to implement an expensive software system, this is an excellent way to quickly and effectively launch a loyalty program.

Gift-of-the-month clubs are another way that product companies can implement a loyalty program. For example, if you're selling children's toys, you could offer a "toy of the month" club where you send a new toy to the customer each month. A chocolatier could create a "Chocolate Club" where they send out a gift basket of different chocolates each month to participants.

Gift-of-the-month clubs are a great gift idea. They are especially popular for birthdays and around the holidays because they're easy gift giving and they're the gift that keeps on giving. It helps you, the entrepreneur, secure money upfront and increase the probability of returning customers. Once a customer's club subscription runs out, you can email them discounts or incentives to rejoin the club. For example, if they have purchased a three-month club subscription, you could send an offer to renew for another three-months and receive the fourth month free.

Advertising

It's important to utilize advertising to explain how your loyalty program works. All of the information about your loyalty program should be conveyed in all of your distribution channels, as well as on your website and social media platforms. This gives you an opportunity to communicate the benefits of the program to both existing and potential customers.

Postcards and emails are also a great way to keep in touch with your best customers... and to inform them about the benefits of your loyalty program. Monthly email newsletters are a very effective form of communication with your best customers, helping to keep your brand on the top of their mind. These newsletters should include information about new products or services, educational information, and special promotions.

Be sure to include a **"Call to Action"** Message, which encourages your customer to act immediately. Possible "call to action" messages could be "Shop Now," "Order Today!" or "Limited Quantities. Call us today." A shoe store could send an email to their best customers announcing the arrival of a limited quantity of new designer shoes, so they (the customer) should "Order Now!" to reserve their size. Or an accountant may send an email to their best customers in January stating that if they send in their taxes before February 15th, they'll receive a 20% discount on their services.

Consistent communication with your best customers helps secure their loyalty, and offering them compelling and seductive benefits with a sense of urgency (call to action) will increase your overall sales.

Services

Most service industries are extremely competitive, and creating a loyalty program will elevate your brand above the competition.

There are a number of different loyalty programs that can be a good fit for service brands. Reminder services are one of the best ways to keep your brand at the forefront of your consumer's mind, while also offering them a value-added service. An appointment reminder service can be implemented via snail mail or email. For example, an esthetician could email her customers about upcoming appointments that have already been scheduled, or she could send a gentle reminder that it's time to schedule an appointment for another facial. Loyalty cards, a points system, or a tier system could also work well for a service business. But remember, you want your loyalty program to be simple for you to execute and easy for your customer to understand. A dog walking service could offer a "blue" loyalty club membership: If a customer spends over $500 a month, they will receive a complimentary grooming. And if they spend over $1000 a month, qualifying them for a "red" loyalty club membership, then they will receive a $150 off coupon, as well as a complimentary grooming.

Websites & Social Media

Since the online landscape is so competitive, loyalty programs can set you apart from your competition. Start by offering free shipping and complimentary gift-wrapping to your loyalty club members, and they will think about your company first the next time they need to purchase a gift online. Even today, many online companies charge for shipping. The word "free" is a very seductive word to many consumers. By offering "free shipping," you're seducing your customers to continue to shop with your brand.

Gift reminder services also work well online. It's easy to collect your customers' information and send them reminder emails with gift ideas. For example, an online gift basket company could create a gift reminder service where they send emails with gift ideas to their customers. This will help their customers save time, which in turn generates a profit for the gift basket company.

Your website and social media sites are wonderful places to encourage customers to sign up for your loyalty program. Place a sign-up link on your home page, and post information on Facebook, Twitter and your blog about your loyalty program, including details about program benefits and how customers can register. You can also set up a "members only" section on your website or Facebook page where you share exclusive information and deals with your best customers. For example, an online children's clothing company could post information on their website, Twitter and Facebook page announcing a special two-hour sale for their most valued customers if they enter a special coupon code during checkout. This will generate immediate revenue for the children's clothing company, while also providing an exclusive discount to their most valued customers.

The Availability Factor

Customers become *Engaged* to a brand because they're able to purchase it easily. So it's imperative that brands retain existing sales channels and expand into new opportunities to make it even easier for customers to purchase the brand. Because their relationship with your brand has become more serious, loyal customers will feel entitled to easy to access your brand.

Since your loyal customers are now in a committed relationship with your brand, it's your job to ensure that they aren't tempted by the competition. One way to do this is to be pervasive in the marketplace, and to be available in all the same places as your competitors. Your Availability should mirror your consumers' shopping habits, so they can easily find you. If they shop online *and* in your retail store, ensure that your brand continues to be available through both of those channels. And you should also research other distribution channels that may benefit your customer in the future.

The Assets Factor

The core features and values of a brand must continue to "wow" or seduce the customer each time they engage in the relationship with your brand. It is usually because the Assets of a particular brand are strong that a consumer remains fiercely loyal to it. However, if at any time the quality of a brand decreases, the customer will quickly exit even a great loyalty program in search of another brand whose Assets better meet their needs. Hence, Assets are also an important Key "A" Factor in this stage.

But again, without an attractive loyalty program encouraging your customers to become engaged to your brand, one slip in quality may cause your customers to quickly exit. At the same time, an attractive loyalty program also gives your brand a second chance in the eyes of many consumers.

Remember, even if a customer is engaged to your brand, you must continue to exceed his or her expectations. The result? A happy customer for life.

THE ENGAGEMENT TAKEAWAY

- Focus on retaining your existing customers by implementing a loyalty program. Remember, it's less expensive to retain existing customers than to constantly acquire new ones.
- Attraction is the most important Key "A" Fac-

tor in this phase, because your loyalty program must be attractive enough to engage your customer and make them forget about the competition.

- Create a loyalty program that is easy to implement and that will motivate your customers to spend more money on your brand.
- Ensure your loyalty program is seductive. Understanding what motivates your customers to shop (upgrades, discounts, free gifts, etc.) will help you to create a successful loyalty program and strengthen the relationship with your existing customers.
- Your loyalty program should have an expiration date. This encourages customers to shop sooner rather than later in order to receive the benefits of their loyalty cards.
- Implement a tiered system where customers must spend a certain dollar amount in order to receive a certain reward. This incentivizes customers to spend more, and it will create additional sales for your company.
- Many retail stores offer exclusive shopping events, personal shoppers and free gift-wrapping services for their best customers.
- Courtesy upgrades are an excellent way to provide exemplary customer service and to make customers feel enthusiastic about their relationship with you.
- Service industries can (and should) send out reminders to their clients about upcoming ap-

pointments that need to be scheduled. Your customers have busy lives, and appointment reminders help to create loyalty because it gives them comfort, trust and reliability with your brand.

Chapter 9

Marriage—Keeping Loyal Customers Happy

Tiffany had always dreamed of getting married on the beach. She and Michael spent months planning their wedding, and exactly one year after their engagement, their wedding day finally arrived. The entire day was magical. Their friends and family were thrilled to witness the ceremony on the pristine beaches of Aruba. Tiffany looked like a princess in her couture wedding dress, and Michael looked dashing in his simple black tuxedo. Although the wedding was small, it was the perfect affair to celebrate their union.

The first two years of their marriage felt like an extended honeymoon. Their love continued to grow as their relationship evolved to a new level. This is not to say they didn't have a few arguments, or "disagreements" as Tiffany liked to call them. However, they found that working through these disagreements only strengthened their relationship. Each day, they worked hard on their relationship and spent a lot of time looking for ways to please one other. Their physical, mental and emotional attraction continued to strengthen. They found comfort in the trust and loyalty they had built in their relationship, and marriage had exceeded both of their expectations.

*   *   *

Marriage between two people represents a strong sense of commitment and loyalty, and similarly, the *Marriage* phase is the pinnacle of the *Dating Lifecycle Curve*, because it represents the point at which customers have invested the greatest amount of time in your brand and have developed the strongest sense of loyalty. Think about those consumers who have been buying the same brands for years... brands such as Coke, Campbell's Soup, Skippy, Wheaties, Charmin and Snickers all have passionate brand loyalists. These brands understand what it takes to retain loyal customers in the *Marriage* phase, and you, as an entrepreneur, can apply these same marketing principles by understanding the strategies used in a successful marriage. These are known as "Retention Marketing Strategies."

> **Love Note:** *The more time a customer spends with your brand, the more deeply they fall in love with you. It's important to treat your loyal customers with sincere appreciation and gratitude, since they represent a large percentage of your overall sales.*

SETTING UP RETENTION MARKETING STRATEGIES

Retention Marketing Strategies encourage your customers to stay "married" to your brand forever.

The loyalty programs discussed in the *Engagement* chapter are the foundation of your retention program. These programs encourage consumers to invest their time and money into your brand over the long-term. The difference between *Engagement* and *Mar-*

riage, however, is the amount of time that a consumer has been loyal to your brand. The more time a customer spends with your brand, the more deeply they fall in love. Remember, it's a lot easier to retain a customer than to find a new one, just as it's a lot easier to stay married than to find a new spouse.

Here are a few important tips to retain a high level of customer loyalty.

Excellent Quality

In order to keep a high level of customer loyalty, it's important to continue providing superior quality in your products or services. Excellence should be the central focus in everything that you do at this stage of the relationship. Many companies become complacent in their relationships with their loyal customers, and as a result, quality may decline. Focusing on quality is important at every phase of the relationship with your customers, but it must be kept at the forefront of your practice in order to keep your customers "married" to your brand. Unfortunately, many businesses make the mistake of only seducing customers at the early stages of their relationship, but it's paramount that seduction continues throughout the *Marriage* phase to keep your customers engaged and in love with your brand.

Product or Service Upgrades

Upgrades are a wonderful way to seduce your "married" customers. By offering upgrades, you show your customers how much you care about the relationship. Loyalty programs should also be upgraded to add specialized features for your very best customers.

Innovation

Since the customer has invested heavily in your brand, they have fallen into a happy and comfortable relationship with you. But it's still important to innovate in order to keep a level of excitement and seduction in the marriage. You can do this by adding new products, new distribution channels, or new marketing vehicles. Innovation can also be applied to your loyalty program in the form of new rewards for your most loyal customers.

Apple and Samsung are two excellent examples of companies who understand the importance of constant innovation. They continue to upgrade their existing products by introducing new products before customers even realize that they need them. Innovation keeps their customers married to their brand because customers want the next "gadget," upgrade or toy that synchronizes with their other products.

Communication

For couples, the key to a happy marriage is communication. In that same vein, the more you communicate with your customers, the more your business will increase. Your communication should be consistent, informational, and educational... but never smothering. Communication could be in the form of emails, newsletters, updates on social media, videos, blog posts, etc. and is integral to your relationship with your customers, because it shows them that you care.

Gratitude

Consider your customers to be a part of your family. Show them that you care by sending thank you cards, birthday cards, preferred customer discounts, free samples, customer appreciation events, and other tokens of appreciation. A new

'VIP' program could be added to your existing loyalty program that offers exceptional benefits and rewards to your most loyal supporters.

Starbucks is a company that understands how important it is to keep their "married" customers happy. They strive for a perfect customer experience each and every time a customer walks through their doors. New flavors of coffee, new foods, new accessories and new services are continually tested in their cafes. Their goal is to exceed customer's expectations by making the best-tasting product every time. Starbucks has also embraced innovation by launching new products such as Starbucks ice cream, Frappuccinos, coffee makers, CD's, breakfast foods, and more.

With their strong customer service orientation, Starbucks makes customers feel welcome. They deliver "attractiveness" in everything that they do. They also strive to show their gratitude to customers with their rewards card, which offers free refills, free food and free drinks. They even have a birthday rewards program, where customers receive a free drink or food item on their birthday.

> **Love Note:** *It's your job to keep the love flowing by implementing retention marketing strategies that involve quality, upgrades, innovation, increased availability, and consistent communication.*

As an entrepreneur, you can apply these concepts to your marketing strategies. "Married" customers have already proven their love and loyalty to you. They have invested a large amount of time with your brand, and it's your job to show them how much you appreciate their loyalty.

> **Love Note:** *Remember, in marketing, it's a lot easier to retain a customer than to find a new one, just as it's a lot easier to stay in a marriage than to find a new spouse.*

MARRIAGE AND THE KEY "A" FACTORS

Let's look at the three Key "A" Factors and how they play into the *Marriage* phase. All three A's—Attraction, Availability and Assets—are important during the *Marriage* phase. A breakdown in any of these factors could lead your customers to engage in an affair, which might eventually end up in a divorce from your brand.

The Attraction Factor

Attraction is just as important in the *Marriage* phase as it was in the *Love at First Sight* phase. Good marriages flourish because couples understand this principle; happy couples keep up their physical appearance and always strive to create a sense of mystery and intrigue. Brands must also maintain their level of attractiveness through a careful balance of consistency and innovation, but customers should still be able to recognize that they are purchasing the same brand because of a consistent use of the brand name and logo. For example, Campbell's Soup has a very identifiable label. It has remained a recognizable—by utilizing the same colors and designs on its packaging—for decades. However, Campbell's is also innovative. They constantly introduce new soup flavors, healthy choices, and robust recipes that use the soup as a base ingredient. Campbell's is a great example of a company that blends brand consistency with innovation, thus keeping their loyal customers "married" to their brand.

Retail Store

In order to keep your "married" customers excited about your relationship, it's important to innovate by introducing new merchandise. This is especially important because the frequency of shopping among your most loyal customers usually increases with time, and they will expect to see something new each time they visit your store. Here are a few things you can do to accommodate them:

- Allocate funds to buy new merchandise each month. Setting a budget will help keep you on track while also increasing excitement in your store by constantly bringing in new and exciting items.
- Move merchandise around your store so it looks as if you've received new stock. For example, if you have a table in the front of the store featuring sweaters, move these to the rear of the store and replace them with t-shirts. Shuffling merchandise weekly helps to keep your store looking fresh and new.
- Buy private label merchandise to create something different from your competition. **Private Label** merchandise is produced by a third party, but sold to a retail business that then adds its own logo in order to create their own line of branded products. For example, *Bella Boutique* could purchase a line of private label candles, to which they could then add their logo: "Bella Boutique Candles."

Products

Married couples understand that adding a excitement to their marriage is an important component of marital success. One way you can improve your product's Attraction during the *Marriage* phase is by creating Derivative Products. A **Derivative Product** is a new product that is an offspring of the original but that has new features, thus essentially making it a new product. Modifying some of your existing products may help to create a level of excitement among your most loyal customers.

Apple, Inc. has consistently evolved their product portfolio to introduce multiple iterations of the iPod, iPhone and iPad. Loyal or "married" Apple customers can't wait for the next generation of their Apple product, and they will often, without hesitation, upgrade to the newest model.

As an entrepreneur, you can follow Apple's philosophy by reviewing your product portfolio to ascertain if there are opportunities for derivative products. For example, if you are selling a line of t-shirts, you could create a new line of shirts made from organic cotton.

Many companies these days are looking for ways to "Go Green" and become environmentally friendly. Launching a "green" version of an existing product not only offers a derivative product, but also helps increase customer loyalty because it demonstrates your commitment to social and environmental responsibility.

Advertising

Consistency in your advertising has yielded strong brand recognition with your "married" customers. At this phase of the *Dating Lifecycle Curve*, it's essential to keep the key elements of your brand image in all of your advertising, while also adding enhancements and innovations to your ads. For example, if you've been running a quarter-page ad in a local magazine, perhaps it's time to upgrade to a full-page ad.

Online marketing can also be upgraded to increase the frequency and distribution of your ads. Perhaps you're only spending $100 per month on Google ads—you could increase this to $200 per month if your budget allows, because it will improve the position of your website in Google's search results.

The essence of advertising is creativity. At this phase of marketing, your customer will appreciate creativity in your advertising if you feature new items, new offers and special announcements. Your ads should continue to improve: better headlines, cooler graphics and eye-catching images.

Remember that Attraction is what first brought your customers to date your brand, and that they "married" you because of their love of the relationship. But in order to sustain that relationship, your advertising needs to continue to be seductive. Again, think about using new headlines and new images to update your ads. Stock images are another option that provides you with professional photos at an affordable rate. Also, websites such as www. Getty.com and www.Corbis.com provide royalty free images that you can use for a specified amount of time. The downside of using stock images is that other companies could be using the same image in their advertising campaigns.

Services

As with products, it's important to take time to review if there are any opportunities to upgrade your current services. Are there any enhancements you could make to your services that will benefit your "married" customers?

The service industry is very competitive, so it's important that your brand continues to innovate. You can launch derivative services that will add a level of excitement to your brand and offer your customers added convenience. For example, a hair salon owner could offer additional services such as facials, nails or massage, thus becoming a day spa as opposed to simply a hair salon. A fitness club could offer nutritional counseling, sports massage, or even open a healthy café in their club. And a catering company could begin offering cooking classes, or eventually launch a cooking school.

It's important to look for opportunities that could expand your current service offerings in order to provide more value to your most loyal, "married" customers.

Websites & Social Media

In the *Marriage* phase, it's important that your consumers' online experience with your brand becomes more exciting. You can do this by adding innovation to your website to make the entire experience easier and more fun. Since your "married" customers use your website most frequently, look for ways to transform their experience. For example, you could update your online checkout process to make it even faster and easier. Or you could launch a new component of your Facebook page where customers can "live chat" with you on the first Monday of each month.

Another option is to begin creating engaging YouTube videos. An image consultant could create videos that explain, for example, how to dress for an interview, first date or special event. Or a company that sells herbs could launch a series of videos demonstrating how to use herbs in everyday cooking.

It's a good idea to periodically review your website and social media platforms. But what can you do to improve your customers' experience? Website enhancements could include new features such as:

- Multiple views of a product
- Gift registry
- Wish lists
- Cross-product promotions
- Online exclusives
- Improved content

Social media enhancements could include new features such as:

- "How to" videos
- Updated images
- Improved content
- Advice
- Contests

The Availability Factor

The *Marriage* phase is an excellent opportunity to expand your brand's distribution channels. If a consumer is "married" to a brand, they will expect that brand to be readily available through multiple distribution channels such as retail stores, outlet stores, ecommerce websites, iPhone apps, catalogs, infomercials, kiosks and selling opportunities through Facebook, eBay, trunk shows, art festivals, flea markets, etc. As an example, a retail store could expand its online presence, develop an iPhone commerce app, and open additional locations.

Pricing during the *Marriage* phase can be difficult. Customers have developed a comfort level with the price that they pay for your brand. And at this point, they have probably already discovered other outlet or discount options that are available. Thus, your ability to raise prices is virtually impossible without alienating some customers. However, due to economic conditions, it may still be a necessity. Loyal or "married" customers will often weather a modest price increase as long as it stays within their expected price zone.

Retail Stores

At this phase in the *Dating Lifecycle Curve*, your customers expect that you'll be available to them anytime, anywhere. Creating special shopping hours for your "married" customers will help solidify their loyalty to your brand. For example, you could create an exclusive shopping event for your VIP customers by opening early or closing late one day. And as mentioned above, you could (and should) continue expanding into multiple channels of distribution. If you have a physical retail store location, be sure you're selling online as well as looking into other channels, such as mobile phone apps.

Product

The *Marriage* phase of the *Dating Lifecycle Curve* is an excellent opportunity not only to expand into new distribution channels, but also to look at different business models. Think about expanding into wholesale, retail, online, new trade shows, mobile apps, Facebook, and more. If you are selling only in the business-to-business market (B2B), now would be an excellent time to sell directly to the business-to-consumer (B2C) market, or vice versa. For example, if you are selling jewelry on the wholesale market through trade shows, perhaps you could consider opening your own retail store, or selling directly to the consumer through a website. It's important to analyze your cost structure to ascertain the feasibility of such a venture.

Creative pricing strategies should be implemented during the *Marriage* phase in order to sustain the passion for your brand that your "married" customers have developed. You could create VIP shopping days where loyal customers receive a discount. Another option is to offer your best customers quantity discounts that encourage them to buy more of your products for a significant discount. Creating a minimum spending threshold, such as "Spend $50 and receive a 10% discount," is a great promotion to offer to your VIP customers.

Advertising

At this point in the *Dating Lifecycle Curve*, you want to be unique and memorable in your advertising campaigns. Consumers love to show that they're "married" to a certain brand by wearing that brand's logo on t-shirts, sweatshirts, hats, etc. So consider designing promotional products with your brand name and logo, because it helps you advertise in a multitude of places each time your customer wears your product. You can opt to sell promotional products such as t-shirts, hats, sweatshirts, tote bags, etc., but I would recommend giving them away to your VIP customers. This is a great way to show gratitude to your customers, and they will feel proud to wear your branded merchandise.

Services

Services can also look for ways to expand channels of distribution—perhaps by opening more locations or offering services in a new venue. For example, an image consultant who works with clients in a local market can expand nationally through the use of Skype or online video tutorials. A dog walking service could hire more staff and thus expand into new communities. And as always, it's important to be easily accessible to your consumers. Perhaps you could add a 24-hour call center (or live chat online) where customers can call in and get help as needed.

Creative pricing strategies work well to keep your customers "married" to your service brand. Keep in mind that your best customers will expect a special discount for their continued loyalty, so your pricing strategies need to balance your profit margins, expenses, and the customer's perceived value. For example, you could create additional incentive programs such as "Spend $100 on your next visit and receive 20% off" or "VIP Tuesdays: Visit us on Tuesdays and receive 10% off your entire purchase."

Ensure that your discount programs benefit both you and your customers. If Tuesday is the slowest day of the week, offer your VIP customers an added incentive for utilizing your service on that day.

Websites & Social Media

It's important to understand your target customers and to know how they shop and gather information. Your "married" customers expect that they will be able to shop with you online through your website 24 hours a day, 7 days a week. Thus you must ensure that all of the images work well on your web pages, that the content is constantly updated, and that the checkout process on your website is easy. Nothing is more frustrating to an online customer (even a loyal customer) than when a website is slow or any information is incorrect.

You can also expand your online Availability by looking into other markets. For example, perhaps you have a large number of Hispanic customers. Giving customers the option to view your website either in Spanish or English may increase the overall number of your customers.

M-commerce (mobile commerce) is something that should be on your radar, if it isn't already. There are many cost effective ways for entrepreneurs to develop mobile apps for their brand, and many web developers now offer, as an affordable add-on, a simple mobile app version of your website.

It's important to view how your website looks on a computer, tablet and mobile phone. Most consumers now use mobile devices to research products and services, and more and more are using it to make purchases. Creating a mobile app for your brand will give your consumers a simple way to purchase your product directly from their phone. Thus your brand will be available to your customers at all times.

Many companies offer different online pricing as a way to entice customers to utilize their ecommerce sites. In order to keep ecommerce shopping exclusive for your "married" customers, you could offer a "flash sale" online. Send your VIP customers an email alerting them about a special online sale between 9 a.m.– noon on a particular day. Include a link in the email that takes them directly to the "flash sale," which is a webpage of special offers for this exclusive, exciting, limited-time event.

The Asset Factor

Consistent product quality and customer service are essential in the *Marriage* phase. Your customers fell in love with you because of your brand's superior quality, durability, taste, reliability and service. In order to sustain a healthy marriage with your customers, it's important to consistently provide excellent products and services throughout the *Marriage* phase.

Seduction never stops throughout the longevity of the relationship with your customers. Deliver superior quality in your products and services, which will show your commitment to the relationship.

Retail Stores

Customers have many choices when it comes to selecting a retail store, but what sets one store apart from another is (1) exceptional merchandise and (2) great customer service. One way to provide outstanding customer service is to call or email your customers when new items arrive. This will make them feel special, and it will help generate sales. You could also improve your return policy by offering your "married" customers a longer return period, or even unlimited returns. In addition, a continued focus on providing superior merchandise will continue to show your "married" customers that you pay close attention to the assets of your brand.

A continued focus on gratitude and customer appreciation is very important in this phase of the *Dating Lifecycle Curve*. It's imperative that you continue the customer appreciation programs that were launched in earlier phases. Communicating your appreciation to your retail store customers may be done through traditional thank you cards sent in the mail or via email. In addition, consistently communicate in-store events, sales and promotions to your customers. They will appreciate your open communication style, and it will make them feel more in touch and committed to your brand. However, be very careful not to over-communicate with your customers; no one likes to get daily spam emails, even from their favorite brands.

Products

Customers will continue to buy your brand based on your product's quality. By offering a first-rate product experience each and every time a customer interacts with your brand, customers won't hesitate to continue their relationship with you. Ensure that you have quality control systems in place to help maintain consistency in product quality, durability and reliability. Your "married" customers expect perfection each and every time they purchase your brand, so it's important to continue making improvements through quality control and product testing.

Maintain your customer appreciation programs to encourage customers to develop an even stronger emotional attachment to your brand. Communication with your most loyal customers may be done through snail mail, email or social media channels. Share information about new product launches, discounts, promotions or special events. And don't be afraid to ask for customer input about new product launches, brand names, recipes, color and flavor selections, etc. This style of communication treats customers as if they're part of your family, and they will become even more invested in the success of your brand.

Advertising

Quality control should extend to your advertising campaigns. Your logo, colors and slogans should remain true to your brand image. For example, if McDonald's changed the color of their logo from red and yellow to pink and green, they would lose significant brand recognition. It would be a disastrous marketing decision!

Consistency is an important component in marriages, and this needs to translate through to all of your advertising programs. Whether you're advertising in a magazine or online, ensure your advertising message is clear and speaks directly to your "married" customers. Always ask yourself, *Does my ad represent the core qualities that my brand provides to my customers?* And remember: Advertising enables you to communicate important messages to all your customers. So review your ads to ensure they appeal to both new *and* existing customers.

Service

Most brands strive simply for customer satisfaction. But you can do better than that. During this phase, you should strive to make customers giddy with excitement about your brand.

For example, customers who stay at the Ritz Carlton are accustomed to five-star service. The hotel offers its customers a complimentary glass of champagne upon arrival, turndown service at night, room upgrades, concierge services, and more. You could provide a five-star experience as well by offering complimentary services to your VIP customers. For example, a drycleaner could offer their best customers complimentary alterations and a 24-hour turnaround. A mechanic could offer their VIP customers faster service, an on-site masseuse or a loaner car. A daycare center could offer their VIP customers complimentary language lessons or after-hours care. Your "married" customers will appreciate these efforts, and thus they'll continue their relationship with your brand.

Service upgrades are another great way to show gratitude to your best customers. Since the service industry is highly competitive, you want to ensure that you remain the first thought in your customer's mind through small but important gestures. Just as it's important for a married man to continue to bring his wife flowers, it's important that you show gratitude by communicating with your customers and continuing to provide stellar loyalty programs and service upgrades.

Websites & Social Media

In order to maintain the excitement in your relationship with your customer, let them feel that they're involved with your brand. **Crowdsourcing** is an excellent way to do this. Crowdsourcing enables your customers to share their ideas about new products, services or content online. Crowdsourcing can be very effective, because it gives you the opportunity to obtain feedback from a large pool of people. And consumers love it, because they feel as if they are part of the team. And it's free!

For example, www.dreamheels.com enables customers to design graphic prints that will be placed on the company's heels. Once a customer creates a design, they upload it onto the website that shows what it would look like on a pair of heels. Then other customers vote on their favorite designs. This is a win-win, because Dream Heels has a large pool of people creating designs, and it's also free advertising, because the "designers" share the Dream Heels website with friends by encouraging them to vote. Customers feel especially involved because they could win a cash award, as well as reap the glory of having designed a new shoe worn by the masses.

As an entrepreneur, you can utilize crowdsourcing to help you develop new ideas for products, services, designs and much more. Your customers will be thrilled to be involved in the process.

THE MARRIAGE TAKEAWAY

- The *Marriage* phase is the pinnacle of the *Dating Lifecycle Curve*, because the customer has invested a lot of time and loyalty into your brand, and now they have fully committed to you.
- Customer retention is the most important part of the *Marriage* phase.
- All three Key "A" Factors— Attraction, Availability and Assets play a vital role in the *Marriage* phase.
- Maintain seduction throughout the *Marriage* phase by increasing the excitement in the relationship with your "married" customers by adding new products, new distribution channels, or new marketing vehicles.
- Implement upgrades and innovations to your products and services to improve Attraction.
- Show gratitude by sending thank you cards, birthday cards, preferred customer discounts, free samples, customer appreciation events, and other tokens of appreciation.
- Proactive communication should be consistent, especially with your "married" customers, because they are the most loyal customers to your brand.
- Expanding your distribution channels increases Availability to your best customers.
- The continued exceptional quality of your Assets will keep your "married" customers in a state of bliss.

- Creative pricing strategies should be implemented in order to sustain the love for your brand by your "married" customers.

- Continue to provide stellar quality products and services to entice your "married" customers to focus on the superior Assets of your brand.

Chapter 10

The Affair—Avoiding Complacency to Retain Loyalty

After five years of marital bliss, things drastically changed when Michael received a promotion at work. His travel increased considerably, and at the same time, his company started going through a corporate take-over. Tensions were high because he didn't know if he would be downsized during the merger. And with increasing time apart, Tiffany and Michael both felt a fissure growing in their relationship.

Ironically, they both started their affairs at the same time. Fortunately, neither knew of each other's indiscretions, so both believed there was still a possibility that they could reconcile their relationship. But when Michael and Tiffany were together, they seemed more like roommates than husband and wife. Their lives had grown routine, and they felt bored in their relationship. The affairs provided excitement and a temporary relief from their daily lives. Deep down they still loved each other, but they no longer knew how to communicate. They knew that if they wanted to repair their relationship, they had a lot of work to do.

*   *   *

There are many reasons why people have affairs: boredom, curiosity and external pressures, to name just a few. But the underlying reason why married couples have affairs is that their needs are not being fulfilled.

By the same token, it's imperative for you to understand that, while some customers may have "married" your brand, it is always possible for their loyalty to waver in an instant.

Just like couples, consumers "cheat" on their favorite brands because their needs are not being fulfilled. For example, if someone has frequent flyer miles with United Airlines, but then suddenly starts flying with American Airlines, it's important to look at the factors that caused them to cheat. Perhaps United didn't have flight schedules that were convenient for the consumer, or perhaps a particular flight was simply full. These types of "unmet needs," whether large or small, can cause a consumer to stray. If United notices a decline in their loyal customer base, they should survey their "married" customers to better understand why they are having affairs. Once they understand that flight times are the cause for the decline, they should then adjust their schedule to meet the needs of their core, loyal customer base.

> **Love Note:** *People cheat on their favorite brands because their needs aren't being fulfilled.*

No relationship is perfect. In marriage, fights and misfortunes occur, which cause discontent. But due to the vows that were exchanged, as well as the time invested in the relationship, many of these fights can be overlooked, and people can "make up" and build stronger relationships in the end.

Communication is key to building a strong relationship. In the case of Michael and Tiffany, Michael could bring Tiffany flowers after a fight, and then sometimes, just on a whim, take her on a romantic cruise for a spontaneous vacation. Because consumers have invested an enormous amount of time in a brand at this point of the *Dating Lifecycle Curve*, they also have an increased tolerance-level for misgivings. Even though customers who are part of your loyalty club program have not taken a literal "vow," they have built up an emotional attachment to your brand. So, if your company has a hiccup— such as out-of-stock merchandise or negative press—many consumers may be able to overlook the mishap. However, in order to repair any damage, clear and consistent communication is imperative. For example, the cable company Comcast has a team that scours Twitter and Facebook for customer complaints, and this team then tries to resolve any issues in order to placate unhappy customers. Not only are customer complaints resolved quickly, but Comcast's brand image is also elevated because other customers witness the company's dedicated focus on their customers.

It's important to be aware of the warning signs of an *Affair* before it happens. When couples first start dating, they go above and beyond to please their partners. But after couples become married, many may feel a false sense of security and become lackadaisical in meeting their partner's needs. As a result, a husband or wife who feels neglected may have an affair with another person merely for companionship and emotional support. Entrepreneurs can learn from this human behavior and never allow themselves, or their customers, to become too comfortable in their relationship.

KEEPING YOUR CUSTOMERS FAITHFUL

Let's be honest: the level of competition in the marketplace today is very high, making it very tempting for consumers to switch brands. It's unrealistic for any entrepreneur to believe that 100% of his or her "married" customers will stay faithful. However, it's still your job to keep as many of your customers as faithful as possible.

You can reduce the number of "cheating" customers by understanding what causes their infidelity. For example, a new brand might have launched into your market with exciting, vibrant packaging. Or another well-known competitor might have lowered prices and caused some of your best customers to switch over.

No matter what the cause, here are some tips to help you avoid an *Affair*:

Communicate

A breakdown in communication is the cause of many affairs. Customers are bombarded with information about your competition on a daily basis. But if you're consistently communicating with your customers, they won't be able to forget you, and the temptation to cheat will be diminished. So be sure to communicate on a consistent basis through emails, newsletters, cards and social media. This involves proactive communication to swiftly and honestly resolve customer complaints.

Love Note: *Communication is a key element in avoiding the Affair. Ensure that you are consistently communicating with your customers, but not bombarding them with extraneous information. Make them feel important, appreciated and loved in all of your communications.*

Survey the Competition

Awareness of your competition is also a critical factor in business. Knowing what your competition is doing will help you to stay one step ahead of them, and to anticipate opportunities to better meet your customers' needs.

Many entrepreneurs foolishly ignore the competition and prefer to live in a bubble. This is very dangerous, because turning a blind eye to your competition will leave you wondering why your customers are cheating on you, and you won't be equipped to make swift and effective changes.

Keep the Relationship Exciting

Companies who fail to innovate are essentially begging their customers to cheat. As mentioned in the *Marriage* phase, it's important to keep the relationship with your customers exciting by launching new products and services that meet your customers' needs. Simple additions, such as upgrades and enhancements, will also add excitement and seduction to your brand and keep your customers loyal.

> **Love Note:** *Innovation will help improve customer loyalty by keeping excitement in the relationship and avoiding customer boredom.*

Focus on Attraction

It's easy for entrepreneurs to get caught up in the daily operations of running a business, and to ignore the "attractive" elements of their brand, such as packaging, logo, the exterior and interior of a retail store, images and information on websites, and social media platforms. Sometimes entre-preneurs launch a great website, but then never go back to update it. You can't let this happen! Do everything possible to keep your focus on the constant improvement of the At-traction of your brand.

Always Be Available

Consumers may cheat on your brand simply because they can't find you. If you are closed, out of stock, or broken down, customers will quickly start looking for an alternative. Ensure that you have systems in place to constantly monitor all dis-tribution channels, so that your brand is always available to customers.

The Price is Right

Affairs could also happen if your competitors offer bet-ter prices. Your "married" customers are loyal to your brand, but they are only human, and they could be seduced by better prices. Be sure to price your products and services so that they are competitive and provide value to your consumers, while still giving you a healthy profit. More importantly, ensure that your best customers are so in love with your brand that price is not their top priority.

> **Love Note:** *Ensure that your "married" customers are so in love with your brand that price is not their top priority. You can do this through compelling loyalty programs and exemplary customer service.*

THE AFFAIR AND THE KEY "A" FACTORS

Lack of Attraction, Availability and Assets could all play a role in causing your "married" customers to cheat. Understand that these customers have a deep sense of loyalty, but that their loyalty could wane in an instant. Focusing on the three Key "A" Factors of your brand will help retain customer loyalty and avoid the *Affair*.

The Attraction Factor

Attractiveness is a quality that can turn heads. Consumers have been conditioned to be attracted to gorgeous brands, especially those that are new and exciting. If a "tall, dark and handsome prince" or a "blonde bombshell" enters the market to compete with a brand that hasn't been updated for years, there will certainly be some attrition to the new, sexy brand. Sad but true, many middle-aged people engage in affairs with someone who is either very young or very attractive. And the "newness" factor, all by itself, is often very appealing.

In order to keep your brand feeling new and exciting, it's important to study your competition. This will help you better understand the temptations that your customers face, and it will enable you to appropriately update the Attraction of your brand. However, you must maintain a balance between innovation and consistency. Loyal customers need to be able to recognize your brand, but you must also continue evolving in ways that keep you attractive.

Retail Stores

The attractiveness of the interior and exterior of a retail store are a big reason why customers continue to shop there.

But it's amazing how many retail stores fail to maintain this aspect of the attractiveness of their brand. For example, I've visited many stores who have not painted the inside or outside of their location in decades. Loyal customers will be tempted to cheat if a new store is more attractive. It's important to paint the interior and exterior of your store every few years. Update the lighting, fixtures, hangers, mannequins and flooring of your store to maintain the attractiveness of your brand. Remember to clean and update your windows on a weekly basis. Mannequins can quickly become outdated or damaged; they should be replaced every few years so they look new and attractive, because they are usually the first thing consumers see when entering your store.

Take time to review your competitors' stores, websites and social media platforms. Analyze their product offerings, store décor, website images, social media content, pricing and advertising. What are they doing differently? How are they seducing your "married" customers? By doing a competitive review, you'll be able to implement changes to better meet your customers' needs.

Products

"Married" customers who are in love with your products could easily cheat on your brand if there is a lot of competition in the marketplace. Even if your customers are not cheating on your brand, it's still a good idea to periodically conduct a competitive analysis.

Review your packaging against that of your competitors. Is it time to update your packaging? Remember, it's important to keep your logo and colors consistent, but there are many ways to update packaging to avoid boredom. Are you still the "blonde bombshell" on the shelf? You can easily increase the attraction of your brand by updating the packaging, hangtags, signage, shipping boxes, displays, etc.

Advertising

The *Affair* phase of marketing gives entrepreneurs an opportunity to analyze their advertising against the competition. Take time to review where your competition is advertising, such as television, postcards, emails, mobile ads, online ads, and any other social media platforms. Next, look at *what* and *how* they're advertising. Are they advertising their product or services with catchy slogans or compelling photography? Or are they using local celebrities to endorse their products? Whatever they're doing, it might be encouraging your loyal customers to engage in an *Affair*. Evaluate your own advertising to ensure that it hasn't become stale and boring. Increasing the attractiveness of your advertising will help you to stay one step ahead of the competition.

Services

Loyalty in service industries is often stronger than that in any other sector. For example, customers will wait weeks for an appointment with their favorite hair stylist. However, if another hair stylist has a more attractive salon or provides creative service offerings, such as a free scalp massage with every haircut, "married" customers may be tempted to cheat with them.

Conducting a competitive review will help you better understand your competition and what sets you apart in the marketplace. Once you understand what makes your competitors attractive to your "married" customers, add services that will better meet their needs and desires.

Websites & Social Media

It's amazing how many companies launch a website and never go back to update it! Building a website is not like building a brick house. It needs to be updated frequently in order for it to continue to be attractive to your "married" customers. Think of your website as a living organism that needs constant care, i.e., changing images, adding new products, updating content, etc.

The most important part of your website is your home page, which is what the customer first sees when visiting your site. Ensure that your home page is always attractive by updating it frequently with gorgeous images and compelling content. Review your competitors' websites to better understand what they are promoting and selling online. Use this knowledge to your advantage, and update your website to promote your competitive advantage online.

The same is true for your social media platforms. Take time to review your competitors' Facebook, Twitter, Instagram, Foursquare, Pinterest, and other pages to better understand what is causing your customers to cheat. Always update your social media with new images, contests, educational information and exciting content that will keep customers coming back for more.

The Availability Factor

Your "married" customers may cheat on your brand out of necessity. If your brand is unavailable, consumers will look elsewhere to find a replacement. Unavailability can happen due to a multitude of reasons, such as your brand being out of stock, your website not working, an employee calling in sick, or inconvenient store hours. These, and other issues, could significantly frustrate your customers. If customers have to work hard to find your brand, they could easily embark on an *Affair* with a competitor who is more readily available.

Pricing is another reason why your "married" customers may cheat. Although price is not the only reason why your loyal customers love you, realistically, it's one of the most enticing factors potentially causing them to engage in an *Affair*. Better pricing is like a beautiful, naked person gliding across the room; you can't help but look! Coupons, sales and discounts are often used by competitors as acquisition vehicles to seduce consumers to try their brand.

Retail Stores

Availability is critical to the success of your retail store. Make sure your inventory is always in stock. If you have products that are flying off the shelves, be sure to reorder early enough so that you don't have any lost sales. And take time to analyze your distribution channels. Are your customers able to purchase your merchandise in a store as well as online? Perhaps it's time to open new locations or to look into new distribution channels, such as wholesale, direct sales, catalog or m-commerce?

Pricing is another critical factor of success for any retail store. Are your products more or less expensive than your competitors? Are you experimenting with any of the creative pricing strategies suggested in the *Marriage* chapter?

The number one reason why you're in business is to make money, so it's important that your pricing strategies yield a profit. However, lower prices or enticing discounts from competitors can cause your "married" customers to embark on an *Affair*. If you notice a decline in your sales or that your regular customers have started to diminish, take time to review your pricing strategies to see if there is an opportunity to incorporate discounts or promotions that are beneficial to both you and your "married" customers.

Products

Products that are out-of-stock can be an impetus to cause your "married" customers to cheat. Try looking for ways to reorder or to expedite the production of your products so that out-of-stock merchandise is never an issue.

Perhaps there are better ways to forecast the number of products you need in any of your distribution channels. Perfecting this system will ensure that your products are readily available wherever your customers might want to purchase them.

Pricing issues can cause havoc in any customer "marriage." Review your competitors' pricing to better understand how they are marketing their products and appealing to your "married" customers. If they are offering more competitive prices, then implement more creative pricing strategies and find ways to convey how your brand better meets the needs of your customers. It's important to remind your customers about your unique competitive advantage, and why you are the right choice versus the competition.

Advertising

Like it or not, customers love coupons, promotions, contests and discounts. These gimmicks give the customer the perception of a lower price or "bargain." In today's marketplace, a lower advertised price is similar to placing a super-model in your advertisements; it helps to get your brand noticed. Competitors will use this marketing strategy by promoting discounts and lower prices through advertising vehicles such as coupons, postcards, emails, flyers, etc. It's your job to ensure that your "married" customers resist this type of marketing enticement. One way to do this is to ensure that your pricing is just as competitive. Conducting a competitive review will help you better understand how to market your unique competitive advantages to your customers.

Services

As with retail stores and product companies, services companies should conduct a competitive review to better understand how they fare against the competition. Review everything the competition is doing, including service offerings, pricing, location, advertising and social media. If you suspect that pricing is a reason why your customers are leaving, survey the competition to better understand their pricing and service offerings. Price is not the main factor why "married" customers cheat, particularly in the service industry, but it does play a role if other parts of your business are not satisfying your customers. Being aware of your competitors' prices will help you create unique pricing strategies that will meet your customers' needs, as well as your sales goals.

Websites & Social Media

It's important that your website is always available to your customers. When websites don't work, consumers usually won't wait around for them to be fixed. If your homepage is down for any reason, it takes a consumer less than three seconds to move on to another website.

Also make sure that all the inventory you sell is available online. There is nothing more frustrating to a consumer who wants to buy merchandise on your website that turns out to be unavailable. Many websites also encounter problems with order process-ing—so check your website daily to ensure that it's working.

By this point of the *Dating Lifecycle Curve*, you should know which social media platforms your "married" customers prefer. If you notice a decline in your core customers, check to see if all your social media platforms are working properly. Many times, images may not be posting properly, or spelling errors and erroneous content could be causing frustration to the consumer. The availability of your brand in the proper so-cial media platforms will ensure that you are seen as a brand that is dedicated to its customers; thus, they will be less likely to cheat, even if your competitors are more accessible online.

The Assets Factor

An *Affair* could result from of a significant decline in a brand's quality, durability or service. Customers often cheat with another brand hoping to recapture the feelings they had on their *First Date* with your brand. So it's imperative that you constantly test your brand's quality to ensure that you are exceeding the expectations of your customers. The qual-ity of your customer service and your ability to address your customers' dissatisfaction will determine whether or not your customers are tempted to cheat with a competitor.

Retail Stores

Any decline in the quality of your merchandise or custom-er service could have an adverse reaction in your "married" customers, so constantly working on improving your store's merchandise and customer service will help you better under-stand why customers may be cheating. Many entrepreneurs fail to develop a strong relationship with their customers, so their customers look to the competition to meet their needs. Since retail is a very competitive business, you should do everything within your power to focus on your Assets and consistently deliver a stellar customer experience.

Products

Any reduction in the quality of your products will have your customers running into the arms of your competitors. It's important to maintain the quality, durability and reliability of your products. A multitude of factors could lead to a change in quality, such as unexpected growth, a change of ingredients, new employees, etc. It's imperative that you maintain quality standards to avoid any decline in the quality of your brand. If you're able to anticipate your customer's needs and articulate this in your product offerings, you will stay one step ahead of the competition, and your customers will not cheat on your brand.

Advertising

Likewise, any decline in the quality of your advertising—such as spelling errors, blurry images or offensive material—will encourage your customers to cheat. Advertising is extremely competitive, and if a competitor's ads are more engaging, enticing or artful, then customers might be willing to try their brand.

Continue to focus on delivering quality advertising while also evolving the copy and images used to fortify your brand image. And always align your advertisements with the unique qualities of your brand.

Services

Have you ever gone to a hairdresser for years, only to walk out of the salon one day with orange hair? If this has never happened to you, count yourself lucky! One horrific experience with a service company will incite many customers into an affair. Sometimes a small mistake could even encourage your most loyal customers to cheat if they are losing their patience with the overall quality of their experience with your brand. Some entrepreneurs become complacent with their "married" customers. But you should treat your loyal customers the same way as you would a new customer, if not better. If a mistake happens, be sure to rectify the situation immediately and offer a complimentary follow-up service so that your customers are not tempted to cheat. Because they have been loyal to your brand for a long time, they will most likely give you the benefit of the doubt and utilize your services again.

Websites & Social Media

Websites and social media platforms change at lightning speed, and it's important to stay ahead of the curve. Many entrepreneurs become overwhelmed with the multitude of tasks that it takes to run a business, and unfortunately, keeping up with social media programs often becomes a low priority. But not updating and maintaining your websites and social media sites can bore your customers, which might lead them to look for another, more stimulating brand experience.

Even though your customers may be "married" to your brand, the ability to have an affair is all too easy in the world of business and marketing. And an affair is even easier online since your competitor's website is only a click away. Ensure that you're delivering consistent and engaging content. This involves checking that all of your images are clear, and that user experience is pleasurable in multiple browsers, as well as on computers, tablets and smartphones.

THE OTHER WOMAN—STEALING CUSTOMERS FROM YOUR COMPETITORS

Sometimes in business, you may want to be *The Other Woman* and seduce customers away from your competitors. In human relationships, the other woman puts on a sexy dress and uses unscrupulous tactics to attract a married man. By no means am I encouraging you to go down such a wicked path, but nonetheless, there *are* a few things to learn from this scenario.

First, ensure that your brand continues to focus on Attraction, so that new customers will take notice. Second, emphasize Availability to ensure that you are located in the right place at the right time in order to entice your competitor's customers. One way to do this is to place yourself alongside your competitors. Or your could offer creative pricing strategies that are so irresistible that new customers are happy have an affair with you. Finally, ensure that your Assets are better than your competitors. Remember: Many customers cheat because of a decline in quality, durability or service. If you are able to outdo your competition and exceed a potential customer's expectations, the customer will be happy to cheat with your brand and hopefully divorce your competitor.

BECOMING "THE OTHER WOMAN"

Becoming *The Other Woman* is not about being unscrupulous. It's about being better than your competitors and exceeding the wants and needs of new customers. Below are a few tips to help you transform your business in order to seduce customers away from your competitors and become *The Other Woman*:

Be Sexy

Ensure that all of your advertising, packaging, store design and anything that the consumer sees about your brand is overflowing with sex appeal. Remember what you learned in the *Love at First Sight* chapter and apply here with new vigor. Become the "blonde bombshell" by ensuring your brand is attractive in every aspect of customer interaction.

Be a Better Communicator

Tempt your competitor's customers with emails, coupons, postcards, online offers, mobile phone offers, and special promotions via apps. One of the reasons that people cheat is a breakdown in communication, so if you are a better communicator than your competitors, you can potentially steal their customers away.

Be Available

Look at which distribution channels your competitors use, and mimic them. Also, you might consider placing your business in close proximity to your competitors so their customers will have an easy time finding you. In some cases, locating your business close to your competition can actually be a good thing.

Be Price Perfect

Discount pricing and coupons are tools used by many competitors to sway unhappy customers to try something new. An increase in competitor's pricing could also encourage their customers to shop around. Look for ways to offer creative pricing strategies to new customers so you increase your availability to them.

Be Fit

Offering exemplary quality, durability, taste and reliability are all reasons why a potential customer may look to experience your brand, especially if their favorite brand is declining in quality. Practicing excellence in everything you do will help seduce your competitor's customers to try your brand for the first time.

THE AFFAIR TAKEAWAY

- An *Affair* is often a result of a breakdown in communication between the brand and the consumer.
- All three Key "A" Factors—Attraction, Availability and Assets could play a role in encouraging your "married" customers to cheat on your brand.
- Focus on the attractive qualities of your brand, and innovate to keep your relationship exciting.
- Analyze the competition to help you better understand why your "married" customers may be cheating.
- Be aware that discount pricing and coupons are tools used by many competitors to seduce unhappy customers into trying something new.
- Ensure your products are always in stock and available for purchase through all of your distribution channels.

- Innovate by launching new products and services that meet your customers' needs.
- Simple additions such as upgrades or enhancements can add excitement to your brand and keep your customers loyal.
- Implement quality standards and uphold them in all facets of your business in order to prevent customers from running to your competitors after one bad experience.
- If you anticipate your customer's needs in order to stay ahead of the competition, then your customers will not be in a hurry to cheat on your brand.
- The consistent quality of your products and services will determine whether or not your customers are tempted to cheat with a competitor.
- Attract new customers by utilizing the tactics of *The Other Woman,* which include being sexy, fit, available, price perfect, and a better communicator.

Chapter 11

Divorce—Looking into the Causes of Failed Marketing Efforts

Michael and Tiffany attended marriage counseling to try to salvage their relationship. But outside of their counseling appointments, they didn't speak to one another and slept in separate bedrooms. Communication had completely vanished. The attraction they had both felt when starting their relationship had quickly dissipated after beginning their affairs. Michael continued to travel with his job, and he purposefully stayed longer on business trips to avoid going home.

After six months of marriage counseling, Tiffany and Michael decided that the best course of action would be to file for divorce. It had been almost six years since their wedding on the beach in Aruba. At that time, neither of them could have imagined that their love would be lost, and that they'd be filing for divorce.

*   *   *

Just like Michael and Tiffany, no one goes into marriage expecting a divorce. Divorce is a tumultuous time in any person's life that leaves them wondering what happened to all of the reasons why they got married. Many books have been written on the causes of divorce. Our purpose is to examine why consumers divorce brands, and how brands can avoid this stage of the *Dating Lifestyle Curve.*

In human relationships, divorce may or may not be caused by infidelity. But in consumers' relationships with brands, infidelity is often the result of brands ignoring their most valued customers. Consumers may "cheat" on their favorite brands because they are bored or don't feel appreciated. Once this dangerous seduction starts with a new brand, consumers could quickly divorce their favorite brands. After all, there is no need for a divorce attorney if a consumer wants to switch brands of ketchup, shampoo or toothpaste.

Embrace Change

In the *Affair* chapter, we saw that loyal customers cheat on their favorite brands for a myriad of reasons. One reason is that customers become bored with brands that don't change. Brands that fail to embrace change and shun innovation will soon end up in the corporate graveyard.

In life as well as in business, the only constant is change. Businesses must continue to innovate in order to keep their "married" customers happy. Eastman Kodak is the perfect example of a company who failed to innovate. They didn't embrace the digital film revolution, and once they realized they had no other choice but to enter the digital marketplace, it was too late.

> **Love Note:** *It's important to embrace change in order to keep your customers involved and happy in the relationship. Seduction is something that should be considered throughout the length of the relationships with your customers, not just in the beginning. Otherwise, you will enter the Divorce phase.*

Anticipate Your Customers' Needs

You must anticipate consumers' every want and need. Through careful consumer study, you can learn which assets need to be enhanced, and thus make any necessary adjustments. Brands that anticipate consumer problems and offer solutions through brand innovation will have a high customer retention rate. On the other hand, brands that remain stagnant will have a high divorce rate, because the competition never sleeps. For example, fast food chains have recently spent a lot of time and money revamping their menus to add healthier options, all without losing their focus on their core product: fast food. By adding salads, yogurts and other "derivative" products, fast food restaurants have successfully broadened their menu to cater to both their existing customer base and to health-conscious consumers.

If you are experiencing a large number of consumers divorcing your brand, it's imperative to ask "Why?" For example, you could ask:

- Has your core product or service recently changed?
- Are there new channels of distribution that could reinvigorate your sales?
- Which advertising vehicles are being utilized to reach your customers?
- Have you recently changed your advertising strategy?
- Are you using the appropriate social media platforms to reach your target customers?
- Are competitors charging better prices or offering discounts to encourage a mass exodus of *your* customers?

- Do you keep your website updated with new images, unique products, and an easy checkout process?
- Has there been a decline in customer service?
- Are your loyalty programs strong enough to keep your customers committed to your brand?
- Are you innovating by adding new products, services and upgrades?

Once these questions are answered, it's essential that you use this information to make changes that will repair the relationship with your customers, and that will prevent future customers from divorcing your brand. By understanding what motivates your customers, you'll be able to develop a stronger relationship with them. It's important to understand what your existing customers like and don't like about your brand, and you can do this with customer surveys and other feedback mechanisms.

> **Love Note:** *Analyze why customers may be divorcing your brand by looking at every aspect of your business. Once you understand why customers are leaving, you'll be able to make changes and repair relationships. Flexibility (i.e., the ability to adapt and change quickly) is necessary to maintain strong, healthy relationships with your customers.*

REPAIRING THE RELATIONSHIP WITH YOUR CUSTOMERS

The difference between an *Affair* and a *Divorce* is that an *Affair* is a short-term relationship that your "married" customers may have with your competitor. During this phase, the customer is still in a relationship with your brand, and you still have an opportunity to repair that relationship.

On the other hand, a *Divorce* is the end of your relationship with customers. They have moved on. You'll know a *Divorce* has happened when there is a steep decline in your sales, and your customer retention rate takes a nose-dive. At this point, you need to focus on how to save your business and stop your other "married" customers from also divorcing your brand. Perhaps you've lost your seduction skills and need to gain them back. In order to do this, you must understand why your customers are divorcing you. Feedback mechanisms should be utilized to help you repair the relationship with your customers.

- A **Survey** is an opportunity to interview a large number of people and ask for their feedback. Surveys may be filled out on a piece of paper or online. There is a great website, www.surveymonkey. com, that enables you to create surveys and query your customers for free. This also provides an online analysis so you're able to obtain results immediately.

- A **Focus Group** is a gathering of six to 12 of your customers where you ask them for feedback about a product, service or advertisement. The benefit of a focus group is that it allows you to speak directly to your consumers. The drawback is that the results are statistically limited, because you are only interviewing a small group of people.

- **Secret Shoppers** can give you information from an unbiased third party to help you better understand the average consumer's experience with your brand. They are paid to go into a store "undercover" and evaluate your brand based on their shopping experience.

> **Love Note:** *Utilize feedback mechanisms such as surveys, focus groups and secret shoppers to better understand what may be causing customers to divorce your brand.*

DIVORCE AND THE KEY "A" FACTORS

The most important Key "A" Factor in the *Divorce* stage is Assets. Although all three Key "A" Factors remain important, it's essential to understand that your brand's Assets are usually the driving force behind losing a loyal customer. Because this customer has been "married" to you for some time, they can usually overlook the surface qualities of your brand (Attraction), and they certainly know where to find you (Availability). But if there is a consistent decline in your brand's quality or customer service—i.e., the foundation of your brand's Assets—then customers will have no choice but to divorce your brand.

The Attraction Factor

In order avoid a divorce, ensure that all aspects of your brand maintain a high level of attractiveness. The focus that you placed on attractiveness during the *Love at First Sight* phase should remain throughout the lifetime of your relationship with your customers. Remember that you are constantly seducing your customers, even in the marriage phase. Otherwise boredom could take over. Your advertising, packaging, websites, retail stores and social media platforms should be enticing to prospective customers, and they should also evolve over time in order to continue to charm your "married" customers.

To keep your relationship exciting and to avoid boredom, embrace innovation. Technological advances have forced brands to embrace change at lightning speed. By being flexible and focusing on the changing needs of your customers, your attractiveness will increase and your divorce rate will diminish.

The Availability Factor

Are customers divorcing products because they can't find them?

It's important that consumers are able to easily access your brand. Perhaps your sales channels are too narrow, restricting the purchasing options for the consumer. For example, if a brand is sold in only one location, consumers may be frustrated if they want to purchase it during off-hours. Or perhaps consumers can't reach your retail store because weather is an issue, though they could easily purchase your brand online… if you had a functioning ecommerce website. If a consumer can't easily find your brand, they may seek alternative brands and begin a relationship with your competitor.

Pricing may also adversely affect the Availability of your brand. If you've recently increased your prices, or if a competitor is offering significantly lower prices with all other attributes being equal, the divorce rate among your "married" customers could skyrocket. If for any reason your loyal customers are dissatisfied with your brand, lower prices offered by a competitor could lead them down the path toward a *Divorce*.

The Assets Factor

As mentioned earlier, it is imperative to understand why the customer is considering divorcing your brand in the first place. What are the specific Assets that could be causing the divorce? Have there been changes in product quality, customer service, or durability that could be causing customers to look elsewhere? If a company is facing a mass exodus of customers, it's important to focus on *why* consumers are choosing to leave, and to implement the findings from surveys and focus groups to stem the tide.

Retail Stores

Feedback on both merchandise and customer service is important to help you ascertain why customers may be divorcing your brand. You can use a suggestion box in your retail store, send out a survey, or host a focus group. Also, hiring a secret shopper will give you unbiased and immediate feedback. They can help you to determine if your store is meeting your customer's needs.

It's also important to review your employee's customer service training. A disgruntled employee with poor customer service skills could cause a number of your "married" customers to begin an *Affair*, which could lead to a *Divorce*. Customer service should be the primary focus of all retail businesses, especially with those who have a lot of direct competition.

It's amazing what a sincere "Hello" and "Have a nice day" can do to help improve your customer's overall impression of your store.

Products

Superior quality, durability and reliability of your products are what originally made your customers fall in love with your brand, so it's important to analyze why your "married" customers are divorcing you. Survey your customers to better understand what's driving them to *Divorce*. You can do this through an in-person questionnaire, snail mail, email, website or social media. The website www.surveymonkey.com is a free, easy-to-use survey tool, and it will provide you with immediate feedback.

Sometimes a focus group works well for product-based companies. Focus groups give you the opportunity to speak to your customers face-to-face. But remember, focus groups only deal with a few people, and their feedback may not be statistically reliable. Still, you might be surprised what you can learn from a well-conducted focus group.

Throughout the process of analyzing customer feedback, it's important to focus on your customer's unmet needs and how to implement changes. Review your products' quality, taste, durability and reliability. And make any changes necessary to repair your relationship with your "married" customers before they divorce your brand.

Advertising

If the competition is advertising more, or if they are designing better ads to seduce your loyal customers, you will see a significant decline in sales.

Surveys and focus groups can also be used to analyze the

effectiveness of your advertising. Survey your customers to see if they like your ads before launching on a larger scale. Perhaps there are different advertising opportunities that could benefit you, such as online advertising, mobile advertising, or other creative advertising solutions (such as wrapping a bus). Advertising can be a huge investment, so it's important to learn what's working (and not working) through customer feedback mechanisms.

Service

Take time to analyze your service offerings to see if there is anything you can improve upon. Customer service also needs to be reviewed, because substandard customer service can push your customers to seek a new relationship. Service companies can utilize surveys, focus groups and secret shoppers to better understand what's working and what's not working. Apply the findings from the feedback mechanisms to make changes that address your "married" customers' unmet needs, and to put the love back into your relationship with them.

Websites & Social Media

Websites and social media are wonderful platforms for surveying your customers, because they are virtually free and provide immediate feedback. You can add a link on your website asking for feedback from your customers. Or you could create a survey in www.surveymonkey.com and place it directly on your Facebook page. To encourage your customers to participate, you could even create a contest around the survey. For example: "Fill out our survey and enter to win a $20 gift certificate."

THE DIVORCE TAKEAWAY

- Divorce can be caused by a myriad of factors, such as poor quality, substandard customer service, lack of innovation, or a breakdown in communication.
- If your brand significantly changes its brand image, or fails to maintain its attractiveness, then customers may swiftly flock to competitors.
- Consistently seduce your customers at each stage of the *Dating Lifecycle Curve*.
- Lack of innovation also opens the door for competitors to encourage a divorce.
- Seduction is something that should be continued throughout the marriage phase so that your customers don't become bored and divorce your brand.
- Assets are the most important Key "A" Factor that lead customers to divorce your brand.
- Survey your customers to better understand their needs.
- Use focus groups and secret shoppers to better understand the Assets of your brand, and swiftly make changes to improve customer satisfaction.
- Keep an open dialogue with your customers, and look for ways to improve your customer service.

Conclusion

Living Happily Ever After

For Jack and Brittany, it was love at first sight. They met at a summer charity event, and an immediate spark of chemistry and intellectual stimulation drew them together. Jack asked Brittany out on their first date and after that, they rarely spent a moment apart. They enjoyed dating, but both knew their love was meant to last a lifetime. Jack met Brittany's parents over the Christmas holidays and proposed to her on Valentine's Day. Brittany had always dreamed of a summer wedding since she was a little girl. Their wedding was like a fairytale, with friends and family celebrating their joyous union.

After two children and ten years of marriage, Jack and Brittany are still madly in love. They make a point of spending time together by reserving a weekly "date" night and by going on an exotic vacation each year to celebrate their anniversary. Times are not always great, but they love and care for one another by being supportive, communicative, and keeping their relationship exciting. They are both grateful for their relationship, and they are looking forward to a lifetime of marital bliss.

*   *   *

Once upon a time, there was an entrepreneur who was seeking a happy life filled with a successful business and loyal customers. That entrepreneur learned about the *Dating Lifecycle Curve*, which helped her appeal to new customers by marketing her brand's attractive qualities, by striving for widespread availability, and by providing products with superior assets. She understood the importance of each stage of romancing her customers, and what it took to keep her customers in a state of marital bliss.

As an entrepreneur, your goal is to reach the *Marriage* phase by successfully courting your customers through the *Dating Lifecycle Curve*. At each phase, Attraction, Availability and Assets play varying roles. But in the end, you want the customer to say "Yes!" when you propose to them… and you want them to fall so deeply in love that they'll never be tempted to cheat on your brand. You want to become the "it" brand in your consumer's mind, so they'll go out of their way to find you, and to buy you.

Marketing any business is a balance between (1) acquiring new customers and (2) retaining your most loyal customers. At the beginning of this book, you learned how to acquire new customers during the *Love at First Sight* phase. What's most important during the acquisition phase is to focus on Attraction and Availability. In human relationships, attraction is the first step in any relationship, and in business, all of your marketing must be emotionally appealing in order to seduce your target customers. All of your advertising, packaging, store design and online platforms should be gorgeous and visually appealing. Once you have created a super-model as your brand image, it then becomes important that your brand is available—in the right place, at the right time, and at the right price.

Asking someone on a first date is extremely stressful, because you never know if you are going to be accepted or rejected. In marketing, you can help to ease this tension by inviting your customer on a date with your brand through coupons, discounts, samples and trial-size offers. Once you've captured their attention, the *First Date* provides the perfect opportunity to "wow" your customers with your brand's incredible Assets.

Quality, taste, reliability and customer service are all extremely important in impressing your customers during the *First Date*, and also to avoid a *One-Night Stand*. Beware of seducing new customers to date your brand through inexpensive pricing. This might label you as "cheap" in the mind of the consumer. And if they don't love the internal Assets of your brand, you might turn into a *One-Night Stand* or "booty call."

The next step in building successful customer relationships is to focus on all three Key "A" Factors as you move into the *Dating* phase. When people first start dating seriously, they may still be seeing a few other people, and they do not have a very strong sense of loyalty. In business, it's your job to show your customers that you are better than the competition by focusing on (1) your strengths and (2) your unique competitive advantage. In order to help your customers forget about the competition, implement customer appreciation programs, such as sending thank you cards and birthday cards. Small gestures go a long way toward your goal of forming long-term customer loyalty.

Customer loyalty truly begins as you enter the *Introduction to Friends and Family* phase. The customer has fallen madly in love with your brand, and they want to share it with their friends and family. Acting as a virtual sales force, these customers will promote your brand through word-of-mouth marketing. Implementing marketing tactics such as discounts, "refer-a-friend" programs, and special shopping events will help to strengthen your relationships with these customers. Attraction and Assets are the primary focus at this stage of marketing, because your brand needs to appeal to your existing customers, as well as to their friends and family.

Loyalty begins to solidify once your customers enter the *Engagement* phase. They are serious about your relationship and will happily make a commitment to your brand. By creating compelling and seductive loyalty programs, you'll encourage customers to further invest in your brand. Loyalty programs are "the engagement ring" that represents your appreciation for your customers' patronage. Attraction is the most important Key "A" Factor in this phase, because your loyalty program must be attractive enough to engage your customers and make them forget about the competition. Be sure that your loyalty programs are easy for you to maintain, while also rewarding your loyal customers with discounts, product upgrades, and complimentary services that will keep them coming back for more.

The pinnacle of the *Dating Lifecycle Curve* is the *Marriage* phase. Every entrepreneur dreams about a long-term relationship with their customers, and the *Marriage* phase represents the point where customers have invested the most time and loyalty into your brand. Consumers in this phase feel comfortable with your brand, and they are very happy in their relationship with you. Your goal during this phase should be to keep your customers happy in their "marriage" by providing excellence in all of your products and services. In order to keep the relationship exciting, it's also important to innovate by upgrading and adding new products, services, marketing platforms and distribution channels. In order to continue meeting your customers' expectations, it's important to focus on all three of the Key "A" Factors. Remember, it's much easier to retain a customer than it is to attract a new one. The more customers who are faithful and "married" to your brand, the more your sales will increase.

Unfortunately, relationships with consumers are more fragile than human relationships. Your customers can easily have an *Affair* on your brand, even if they're "married" to it. That's why building customer loyalty is extremely important. Customers who feel their needs aren't being met will be tempted to cheat on your brand. If you are able to be flexible and make changes as your customer's needs change, you'll be able to continue on the road towards marital bliss and avoid the *Divorce*.

So... the moral of the story is simple: Remember that seduction occurs throughout the lifetime of the relationship with your customers, not just in the beginning. Therefore, keep your customers happy by meeting their needs through innovation, communication and appreciation. Loyalty is something that is earned through hard work and dedication.

And it's worth it! Because once you and your loyal customer are happily "married," you'll both ride off into the sunset.

Glossary

Acquisition: Strategies utilized to acquire a customer for the very first time. Customers will have their first experience with a brand during the acquisition phase.

Advertising: Promoting a business through magazines, television, email, social media, the Internet, billboards, etc. In order for a company to "advertise" they must pay a fee to have their brand featured in the desired location.

Assets: The internal attributes of a brand that meet a customer's need. Examples of a brand's assets include reliability, durability, service, taste, quality and value. Assets are one of the Key "A" Factors.

Attraction: The physical attributes of your brand. Attraction applies to all external aspects of your brand, including package design, advertisements, signage, social media sites, websites, apps, catalogs, retail store designs, billboards, event marketing and public relations campaigns. Attraction is one the Key "A" Factors.

Attributes: Physical criteria that the advertising industry has deemed as attractive and sexy.

Availability: This involves both the location and the price points of a brand. Products or services must be available to the consumer at the appropriate location and at the right price. Availability is one of the Key "A" Factors.

Brand: Something that identifies your product, service or company such as a name, word, logo or design.

Branding: The process of creating and developing your company's image over time.

Brand Image: The personality of the brand as perceived by the consumer. What the consumer thinks about a brand.

Booty Call: Consumers who occasionally purchase a brand because it is cheap and their choices are limited. A Booty Call is not a consumer's first choice. The lower price point may enable consumers to come back again, but they will forever label the product as "cheap" and as their very last resort. Not a long-term strategy.

Call to Action: A marketing message that encourages the customer to do something within a certain time period. It creates a sense of urgency.

Derivative Product: A new product that is an offspring of the original and has new features that make it into a new product.

Distribution Channels: Any point of sale opportunity including retail stores, outlet stores, ecommerce websites, iPhone apps, catalogs, infomercials, kiosks, selling opportunities through Facebook, eBay, trunk shows, art festivals, flea markets, etc.

Childhood Brand Loyalists: Consumers who are loyal to a brand because they associate it with their childhood.

Competitive Advantage: The features and benefits of your brand that make you better than the competition.

Competitive Analysis: This reviews your business offerings against the competition. It's important to review at least three competitors and analyze their products, services, pricing, location, advertising, websites and social media programs.

Critical Point: Turning point or fork in the road where the consumer will make a decision.

Crowdsourcing: An online forum that engages customers or a "crowd" to offer feedback, advice and support on an existing project or idea.

Dating Lifecycle Curve: The Dating Lifecycle Curve illustrates the stages that people fall in love are parallel to the way marketing programs should be implemented in order to increase customer loyalty. Consumer's reactions to advertising and marketing programs can be inferred to their reactions to the Dating Lifecycle Curve. The graph shows that the longer a customer "dates" a brand, the more their loyalty increases.

Distribution Channel: An avenue for businesses to sell their products or services to the consumer that include the Internet, retail stores, catalogs, social media, mobile application, home shopping networks, direct selling, etc.

DNA: The DNA of your brand is represented by the key elements of your brand. For example, the DNA of McDonald's could be fast, convenient and cheap.

End Cap: A display opportunity for products to be showcased at the end of an aisle. This is a prime selling space for many products as the customer comes into contact with them head on, and they have few other products competing for their attention due to the narrow shelving options at the end of an aisle. Normally, one to three products are displayed on an endcap at any one time.

Focus Group: A group of six to 12 of your customers used for gathering feedback about a product, service or advertisement.

The benefit of a focus group is that it allows you to speak directly to your consumers. The drawback is that the feedback can be of limited value because you are only interviewing a small group of people.

Innovation: Doing something new. Launching a new product or service that is different from anything else in the marketplace and fulfills the needs of your customers. Sometimes consumers are unaware of these needs until they learn about a new product/service that solves a problem or enhances their lives.

Key "A" Factors: ATTRACTION, AVAILABILITY and ASSETS are the Key "A" factors. At different stages of the *Dating Lifecycle Curve*, one or two of the three "A's" will become more prevalent over the others. The A's that are most important at each phase are referred to as the Key "A" Factor(s).

Marketing: Selling an image through various "channels" such as the Internet, emails, social media, retail, catalogs, home shopping television networks, etc.

Place: Location, location, location. For products, the place could be a channel (retail, Internet or catalog), store location, shelf space within a store, end cap or POS display. This could also be the media channel for promotions: television, direct mail, outdoor advertising, event marketing, retail marketing or radio.

Pay Per Click: You pay each time a consumer clicks on your ad. Companies such as Google AdWords, Google AdSense and Yahoo Search Marketing offer this service.

Pay Per Impression: You pay each time your banner ad "pops up" on a web page.

POS: Point of Sale. A sales promotion that is at or near the cash register or check-out.

Price: The price at which a product or service sells for in the marketplace.

Price Point: The suggested price at which to sell your products or services while taking into consideration your competitor's prices.

Price Zone: The elasticity of price points that consumers will feel comfortable paying. This helps you to calculate the highest and lowest prices that you can charge for your products and/ or services.

Private Label: Merchandise that is sold to a business who adds their logo to create their own line of branded products.

Product: A tangible item that is produced and sold.

Profit: Any money that is left over from overall sales after deducting the expenses needed to bring the product to market. (Profit = Sales – Costs)

Profit Margin: Calculated by the dividing the profit by the sales. (Profit Margin = Profit/Sales)

Promotion: Any vehicle that enhances the creativity of a product or service. Promotion could entail: package design, advertising, signage, catalogs, direct mail campaigns, billboards, event marketing or public relations campaigns.

Response Rate: The number of people who respond to a form of communication, such as a postcard, brochure or email.

Retention: Strategies to keep (retain) a customer purchasing a product for multiple purchases. A customer becomes a repeat customer in the retention phase.

Retention Marketing Strategies: Tactics that encourage your customers to stay "married" to your brand. For example, loyalty programs are designed to give consumers a reason to stay in a relationship with your brand.

SEO: Search Engine Optimization. These are tactics used to assist in a high-ranking placement of your website by the search engines. Experts in this area work on your website so that key words, page titles and image descriptions help to boost your website higher in the search engine rankings.

Secret Shoppers: People who are paid to go into a store "undercover" and survey your brand based on their shopping experience.

Sponsored Search Engine Ads: You pay to have your website appear in the top portion or "sponsored links" section of search engines such as Google, Bing and Yahoo.

Survey: An opportunity to interview a large number of people and ask for their feedback. Surveys may be paper-based or completed online, which is a much easier way to gather and analyze feedback.

Target Customer: People who will most likely buy your products and services. Businesses should focus their marketing efforts to attract this group of potential customers.

Trunk Show: An event where designers promote their newest merchandise inside a retail store.

Viral Marketing: Word of mouth marketing online. This moves at warp speed due to numerous people reposting, retweeting, etc.

Wholesaling: The selling of merchandise to a retailer or vendor who then marks up your product and sells it to the end consumer.

About the Author

Kerry Szymanski is a full-time Professor of Fashion Merchandising at the Art Institute of Fort Lauderdale, where she received the "Honored Faculty of the Quarter" Award in June 2013. Szymanski is also the president of Kerry Communications—a marketing consulting firm. With over twenty years of industry experience, Szymanski shares her extensive knowledge and experience of business planning, marketing, branding, strategic planning, PR, social media, production planning, business coaching and design creation with entrepreneurs. Ms. Szymanski is a professional speaker who lectures about marketing and branding throughout the country.

Szymanski's background integrates entrepreneurship with corporate marketing experience. In 2004, she launched SassyBB, a design-your-own purse boutique in Fort Lauderdale, Florida. Her corporate experience includes retail as well as direct and Internet marketing for companies such as Bally Total Fitness, Harry and David, and Duty Free Americas. She holds an MBA from the University of Oregon and a BA in International Relations and French from Syracuse University. In 2009, *Gold Coast* magazine voted Szymanski one of the "40 under 40" rising business stars in Broward County. She has been featured in local and national magazines, newspapers, and television programs. Professor Szymanski resides currently in Fort Lauderdale.

CPSIA information can be obtained at www.ICGtesting.com
Printed in the USA
BVOW08s0123260215

389438BV00004B/16/P